PONS

Wolfgang Hohlbein
Fight of the Dragon

PONS GmbH
Stuttgart

PONS

Wolfgang Hohlbein
Fight of the Dragon

Englisch von Brian Melican

1. Auflage 2011

PONS Produktinfos und Shop: www.pons.de
PONS Sprachenportal: www.pons.eu
E-Mail: info@pons.de

Englische Übersetzung, Annotationen und Übungen: Brian Melican
Redaktion: John Dalbey
Projektmanagement: Mareike Geib
Logoentwicklung: Erwin Poell, Heidelberg
Logoüberarbeitung: Sabine Redlin, Ludwigsburg
Sprecher/Tonaufnahmen: Dave Hickman, UK
Layout: Petra Michel Gestaltung & Typografie, Bamberg
Satz: Satzkasten, Dollenbacher & Müller, Stuttgart
Coverillustration und Einbandgestaltung: hilden_design, München
Druck und Bindung: Print Consult GmbH, München

Printed in Czech Republic.
ISBN 978-3-12-010072-0

Inhaltsangabe

Timucin und sein Schwurbruder Chuzir sind allein. Ohne Unterstützung schlagen sie sich durch den eisigen Winter der Steppe, auf der Flucht vor dem grausamen Stamm der Tajin. Endlich scheint die Rettung nah: Timucins Mutter, begleitet von einigen Kriegern, findet die beiden nach monatelanger Suche.

Gerade als die Gefahr vor den feindlichen Kriegern gebannt scheint, greifen die Tajin an! Nur mit Mühe können Chuzir, Timucin und die Krieger seiner Mutter die Feinde in einem erbarmungslosen Kampf zurückdrängen. Chuzir wird dabei schwer verletzt – doch erstmal bleibt keine Zeit, seine Wunden zu versorgen. Zunächst müssen sie einen sicheren Unterschlupf finden. Sie verschanzen sich auf dem Gipfel des Heiligen Berges. Doch von dort führt nur ein Weg hinab, und dieser wird von den Tajin belagert!

Immer wieder kommt es in dieser brenzligen Situation zur Konfrontation zwischen Timucin und Ilhan, seinem alten Feind, der nun angeblich treu zu Timucins Mutter steht. Doch ist das die Wahrheit? Als Chuzir trotz seiner schweren Verletzungen plötzlich verschwindet, kommt es fast zum Kampf! Wie durch ein Wunder fliehen die Tajin plötzlich Hals über Kopf. Doch weshalb? Timucin findet es bald heraus und muss sich schließlich einer schweren Prüfung unterziehen, die sein ganzes weiteres Leben beeinflussen wird.

Auftretende Personen

Timucin

Timucin sollte der Khan der Kijat sein, des Klans seines Vaters. Doch seit einem feigen Verrat ist sein Klan in alle Winde zerstreut und er selbst geriet in Gefangenschaft. Sein bester Freund und Schwurbruder Chuzir befreite ihn jedoch und steht nun treu zu ihm.

Chuzir

Der tapfere Chuzir ist Timucins Schwurbruder, sein bester Freund und enger als ein leiblicher Bruder mit ihm verbunden. Dennoch war er gezwungen, Timucin zu verraten, sodass dieser in Gefangenschaft geriet. Doch Timucin vertraut ihm noch immer voll und ganz.

Sarantuya

Timucins geheimer Traumdrache Sarantuya hilft Timucin in schweren Zeiten und steht ihm mit dem weisen Rat der Drachen zur Seite. Doch es gibt auch eine starke Versuchung für Timucin: Er kann Sarantuya befehlen, alles für ihn zu tun – selbst die schlimmsten oder grausamsten Taten. Doch dann würde er Sarantuya für immer verlieren!

Üdschin

Üdschin ist Timucins Mutter und zurzeit die Khanin von Timucins Klan. Das ist sehr außergewöhnlich, da sonst nur Männer das Amt des Khans inne haben. Sie hat sich auf die Suche nach Timucin gemacht, um ihn aus der Gefangenschaft zu befreien. Nun unterstützt sie ihn, damit er nach ihr das Amt des Khans über die Kijat übernehmen kann.

Ilhan

Ilhan ist etwas älter als Timucin und sein ärgster Feind, seit sie kleine Jungs waren. Zusammen mit seinem Vater hat Ilhan den Sturz Timucins betrieben, der nach dem grausamen Tod seines Vaters eigentlich hätte Khan werden sollen. Jetzt steht Ilhan aber angeblich treu zu Üdschin, Timucins Mutter.

Udugur
Er verkörpert die lang ersehnte Unterstützung für Timucin und seine Mutter: Udugur, der Kriegsherr der Merkiten. Er ist der Onkel von Timucins Mutter. Er ist bereit, Timucin gegen die grausamen Tajin zu beschützen – doch diese Hilfe hat ihren Preis!

Arbesa
Arbesa ist Timucins Verlobte – oder war es einmal. Sie wurde in die Gefangenschaft verkauft und hat Timucin nun seit fünf Jahren nicht mehr gesehen. Er fühlt immer noch dieselbe Liebe zu ihr wie früher. Doch wie ist es bei ihr?

WOLFGANG HOHLBEIN

FIGHT OF THE DRAGON

The Prophecy

TR. 01

So Timucin has become khan[1], even though it did not happen the way he wanted it to. His father is dead. He was betrayed[2] and murdered by people he had trusted[3] and risked his life for. His mother has disappeared[4] and his tribe's[5] livestock[6], lands and belongings[7] have been stolen and divided amongst enemies. The tribe's few remaining warriors[8] have taken their families and fled[9] in all directions. Timucin would not have wished this on his worst enemy. The worst thing is that Arbesa, the only person in the world whose life is more important to him than his own, has been sold as a slave – and it is all his fault[10]. Only Chuzir is left from among the small group of men that came to rescue him – and you can't really call Chuzir a man. He is really nothing more than a boy, not much older than Timucin himself.

But Timucin is khan, though, and isn't that what he has always wanted? Of course, he never imagined he would be khan of a tribe, consisting just of two men. But when has fate[11] ever cared much about the desires of men, let alone[12] their exact wishes about *how* things should happen.

Perhaps fate does care, though, and you men have forgotten how to hear its voice?

1 **khan** – *Khan (Häuptling eines Steppenvolkes; im Englischen wird* khan *nur in der Anrede groß geschrieben. Z. B. „Forgive me, my Khan!")*
2 **betrayed** – *verraten*
3 **to trust sb** – *jdm. vertrauen*
4 **to disappear** – *verschwinden*
5 **tribe** – *Sippe, Stamm, Klan*
6 **livestock** – *Vieh*
7 **belongings** – *Besitz, Hab und Gut*
8 **warrior** – *Krieger*
9 **to flee, fled feld** – *fliehen*
10 **all his fault** – *allein seine Schuld*
11 **fate** – *Schicksal*
12 **let alone** – *geschweige denn*

Timucin ignores the silent whisper[1] in his thoughts and puts up the hood[2] on the warm jacket that Chuzir had to almost force him to wear[3]. He is just able to resist the urge[4] to rub[5] his hands together or blow into them to warm up the most frozen parts of his fingers. He has to try even harder to not stamp his feet. These things could help him to forget how cold he is, but it would not be appropriate[6] to a great khan.

Don't you worry, little Khan. No one can see how the man who will later rule the world is standing here now, with his teeth chattering[7] from the cold.

As ever, Sarantuya's voice whispers straight into his mind[8]. Something in her voice seems to taunt[9] him and scares him at the same time.

"Well, even if nobody can see it, a place like this is not worthy of[10] such a gesture," answers Timucin grumpily[11]. His voice, however, is so weak and trembling[12] that it sounds like that of a new-born baby.

A place like this, repeats Sarantuya at the back of his mind. *You mean this lonely place at the very end[13] of the world? A place so miserable[14] that even most animals avoid it? A place at which there is nothing, nothing worth coming for at all?*

"That is not true," protests Timucin. "This is a sacred[15] place!" He speaks passionately[16]. He wants his words to sound impressive[17], but his lips

1 **silent whisper** – *lautloses Flüstern*
2 **hood** – *Kapuze*
3 **he had to almost force him to** – *er musste ihn fast dazu zwingen*
4 **to resist the urge to** – *dem Wunsch widerstehen*
5 **to rub** – *reiben*
6 **to be appropriate to a khan** – *eines Khans würdig sein*
7 **to chatter (teeth)** – *klappern (Zähne)*
8 **mind** – *Gedanken, Geist*
9 **to taunt** – *verhöhnen*
10 **to be worthy of sth** – *einer Sache angemessen sein*
11 **grumpy** – *mürrisch*
12 **trembling** – *zitterig*
13 **at the very end** – *ganz am Ende, am äußersten Ende*
14 **miserable** – *armselig, elend*
15 **sacred** – *heilig*
16 **passionately** – *leidenschaftlich, inbrünstig*
17 **impressive** – *beeindruckend*

are so numb[1] with cold that he can hardly move them. Sarantuya does not answer at all. Timucin decides to compromise between his pride[2] and the danger that he might actually freeze. He sticks his hands in his armpits[3] and then stamps off through the thick snow. He walks around the tall rocks and has a clear view of the land on the other side. But the view isn't any better there, because the snow is still falling. Everything is covered in a grey-white blanket. There is nothing to see but shifting shadows and falling snowflakes.

The dragon is right, of course, and Timucin knows it. It is so cold up here that nobody can stand[4] it for more than a few short hours. But Sarantuya is also wrong, because this place *is* holy[5].

Only because you men have called it holy and are too proud[6] to admit[7] that you might have made a mistake? scoffs[8] Sarantuya.

This may be the case for some people, thinks Timucin. But it is not true of[9] him. He *knows* that this place is holy. This is the place where he saw Sarantuya for the first time. He knows her voice for as long as he can remember[10], but the first and only time he ever actually saw the dragon was here. Perhaps the place isn't holy, but it certainly is magical[11], whatever the difference might be.

Timucin takes a few more steps, going right to the edge of the cliff. Carefully[12], he crouches[13]. His joints[14] crack like an old man's. Even though he cannot see the edge of the cliff, he is sure he is very close to it. He wants to

1 **numb** – *taub, betäubt*
2 **pride** – *Stolz*
3 **armpit** – *Achsel*
4 **to stand sth** – *etw. aushalten*
5 **holy** – *heilig*
6 **proud** – *stolz*
7 **to admit** – *zugeben, eingestehen*
8 **to scoff** – *spötteln*
9 **to be true of sb/sth** – *für jmd./etw. gelten, zutreffen*
10 **as long as he can remember** – *solange er denken kann*
11 **magical** – *magisch, verzaubert*
12 **careful** – *behutsam, sorgfältig*
13 **to crouch** – *in die Hocke gehen*
14 **joints** – *Gelenke*

grab[1] on to one of the jagged[2] rocks next to him, but his pride[3] stops him. Before Sarantuya can say anything, he realises how stupid he is being.

Not to mention how dangerous this is, adds Sarantuya, of course.

Timucin ignores[4] her. He grabs one of the ice-cold rocks with his left hand. His eyes are burning from the cold wind, but he tries to see through the grey mist[5] into the valley. A gust of wind[6] roars up from below, playing with the fur[7] of his hood. His teeth start chattering, he can't stop them.

Who are you trying to impress[8] by doing this little Khan? whispers Sarantuya in his thoughts. *Except for yourself.*

Timucin doesn't answer, but just bends[9] forward a little further[10] and tries even harder to see into the pale[11], snowy fog. The light is fading[12]. He tries to remember the first day he climbed to the top of Burchan Chaldun. It was about five years ago, but so much has happened that it seems ten times longer[13]. His life has changed a lot since then, and so has the view from up here[14]. Back then[15], the country below him opened up into endless plains[16], dotted with thick forests and green meadows[17] that made good hunting and riding[18]. There were evergreen pastures[19], crystal clear

1 **to grab on** – *greifen nach, festhalten an*
2 **jagged** – *gezackt, scharfkantig*
3 **pride** – *Stolz*
4 **to ignore sb** – *jdn. missachten, nicht beachten*
5 **mist** – *Nebel, Dunst*
6 **gust of wind** – *Windstoß, Windböe*
7 **fur** – *Pelz*
8 **to impress** – *beeindrucken*
9 **to bend forward** – *vorbeugen*
10 **a little further** – *ein bisschen weiter*
11 **pale** – *hell, blass, bleich*
12 **the light is fading** – *es dämmert*
13 **It seems ten times longer** – *Es kommt ihm zehnmal so lange vor*
14 **and so has the view from up there** – *ebenso wie der Blick von dort oben*
15 **back then** – *damals*
16 **plain** – *Ebene*
17 **meadow** – *Wiese*
18 **to make good hunting and riding** – *zum Jagen und Reiten einladen*
19 **evergreen pastures** – *unerschöpfliche Weidegründe*

streams[1] and shady groves[2]. In those days, he could see the hazy outlines[3] of further mountains, perhaps even higher than the one he is on now.

Now, there is nothing but an endless, grey sea. Grey shadows seem to move and dance in the unending nothingness[4] in front of him. Perhaps this place is not magical at all, but it certainly can make people see things that aren't there.

Either that, or it is able to hide things that are *there, little Khan. Then again*[5]*, one way or the other, it's all the same*, says Sarantuya with a gentle dragon laugh. *I don't think I'll ever understand you humans. Your whole existence is based on your senses*[6] *but you do not trust them at all.*

Timucin could say quite a lot in reply[7], but he is not in the mood[8] for a philosophical discussion with a dragon – a dragon that he is not at all certain actually exists.

I could take offense[9] *at that,* replies Sarantuya, *what else do I need to do to prove that I exist?*

You could help me, answers Timucin silently, although he knows what Sarantuya will most likely say to this.

She doesn't disappoint: *But you already have all the answers, little Khan.*

So you mean that I still need to find the right questions, then? says Timucin, bending[10] even further forward until he almost loses his grip[11] on the icy rocks. The sun has almost disappeared behind the mountains and it will be completely dark soon. Instead of staying here and possibly risking

1 **stream** - *Bach*
2 **shady grove** - *schattiger Hain*
3 **hazy outline** - *verschwommener Umriss*
4 **nothingness** - *Nichts*
5 **then again** - *andererseits, schließlich*
6 **senses** - *Sinne*
7 **He could say quite a lot in reply** - *Er könnte vieles antworten*
8 **to be in the mood for sth** - *der Sinn nach etw. stehen*
9 **to take offense at sth** - *sich von etw. beleidigen lassen*
10 **to bend forward** - *sich vorbeugen*
11 **to lose one's grip** - *seinen Halt verlieren*

his neck[1], he really should be heading back[2] down the mountain while he still can. Instead, he leans further forward.

A stone comes loose[3] from under his feet and falls into the abyss. Suddenly, Timucin's reason[4] proves to be stronger than his defiance[5] – he crawls back from the brink[6]. Once he is a good way back from the edge, he stands up. He is disappointed[7], although he knew what he would see here[8]. He knew that his path[9] would end here – after all, they don't say that the world ends here for nothing[10].

Aren't you the one who is always saying that what "they" say doesn't matter?

Timucin is definitely not in the mood to answer a question like that. In fact, he thinks, this dragon only really tells him what he already knows in any case.

That, and what you are too scared to admit[11].

TR. 02

At this moment, Timucin would like to have a voice in his head that says nice, encouraging[12] things. After all, the bony fingers[13] of despair[14] are knocking on the door to his mind. Perhaps this isn't the end of the world as such, but almost certainly the end of his path. They can flee no further[15].

1 **to risk one's neck** *(Redewendung) – Kopf und Kragen riskieren*
2 **he really should be heading back** – *er sollte wirklich zurückgehen*
3 **to come loose** – *sich lösen*
4 **reason** – *Vernunft*
5 **defiance** – *Trotz*
6 **brink** – *Kante*
7 **disappointed** – *enttäuscht*
8 **although he knew what he would see** – *obwohl er wusste, was er sehen würde*
9 **path** – *Pfad, Weg*
10 **They don't say it for nothing.** *(Redewendung) – Sie sagen das nicht von ungefähr.*
11 **to admit** – *zugeben*
12 **encouraging** – *aufmunternd*
13 **bony fingers** – *dürre, knochige Finger*
14 **despair** – *Verzweiflung*
15 **They can flee no further** *(veraltet) – Ihre Flucht endet hier*

"It definitely will be the end of you if you just stand around here doing nothing," growls[1] the dragon. For the second time in all his years with Sarantuya, this is the second time he actually hears her voice outside of his thoughts. Instead of silent whispers in his mind, the dragon is audibly[2] growling.

If there is one creature[3] on this earth that he has no need to fear, it is his dragon. Nonetheless, his heart starts to beat wildly[4] as the golden, scaled[5] figure appears. She is bigger than the biggest of yurts[6] and more beautiful and more dangerous than anything he has ever seen. Her eyes are at once soft like a doe's[7], but they burn into his soul like fire.

"Why did you call me to this place, then?" asks Timucin directly, his heart beating faster than ever before.

"I? Call you here?" Despite the fact that Sarantuya has the face of a dragon and not a human, she still manages to look clearly surprised. "It was your decision to come here, little Khan!"

Timucin wants to reply that he is not in the mood for this kind of silly game[8], but the scornful sparks[9] in Sarantuya's eyes silence[10] him. Just as he has always heard the dragon's voice in his mind, the dragon always knows what his thoughts and wishes are.

Even those that you do not know about[11]*, little Khan.*

Something about these words, now silent again, scares him. He can't say what it is – perhaps he is just afraid of the answer. He looks at Sarantuya's face for a few moments, before turning around and looking to the North. In the short time he was talking to the dragon, his surround-

1 **to growl** - *knurren*
2 **audibly** - *hörbar*
3 **creature** - *Geschöpf*
4 **to beat wildly** - *wild klopfen*
5 **scaled** - *geschuppt*
6 **yurt (tent)** - *Jurt (Zelt)*
7 **doe** - *Reh*
8 **silly game** - *Spielchen*
9 **spark** - *Funke*
10 **to silence** - *zum Schweigen bringen*
11 **even those that you do not know about** - *selbst die, die nicht einmal du kennst*

ings have changed. The snow is still falling and the grey fog is still lying over the land like a cloak[1]. It is difficult to make out[2] shapes, or even see where the sky goes into the ground. Timucin turns around to look for Sarantuya, but the dragon is gone. The snow keeps falling[3] and starts to cover the dragon's tracks[4].

Instead of the dragon, a figure emerges[5] from the silent swirls of snow and mist[6]: A slim[7] girl with long, black hair and a smooth[8] face with powerful features[9] and dark eyes. Before he knows it, Timucin has lost himself in these eyes.

He knows that it can't be Arbesa: she is a thousand miles away, another world away. Nonetheless, he becomes anxious[10] and feels guilty. Why is the dragon sending him this awful vision?

Because I am going to lose you, little Khan, answers Sarantuya, using Arbesa's voice, and not moving her lips. *I can feel it.*

"Rubbish!" replies Timucin, almost shouting, "I would never…"

It's not your fault, interrupts[11] the dragon, once again silently using a booming voice[12] in his thoughts. *If you men were able to use the power of the dragon as you should*[13]*, then we would never have left you.*

"But I have never abused[14] you," protests Timucin.

Why is the dragon saying this? Hasn't Timucin proved that he is strong enough to resist the temptation[15] of absolute power? Back when he

1 **cloak** – *Mantel*
2 **to make sth out** – *etw. erkennen*
3 **to keep falling** – *weiterhin fallen*
4 **tracks** – *Spur*
5 **to emerge** – *heraustreten*
6 **swirls of snow and mist** – *Wirbel aus Schnee und Nebel*
7 **slim** – *schlank*
8 **harmonious** – *ebenmäßig*
9 **powerful features** (*hier*) – *ausdrucksstarke Gesichtszüge*
10 **anxious** – *beklommen, ängstlich*
11 **to interrupt** – *unterbrechen*
12 **booming voice** – *dröhnende Stimme*
13 **as you should** – *wie es sich gehört*
14 **to abuse** – *missbrauchen*
15 **to resist temptation** – *eine Versuchung widerstehen*

and Arbesa returned to the camp to discover his father murdered and the clan betrayed, he could have unleashed the full fury of the dragon[1] and crushed[2] those who had done this to him. What else does he have to do, to prove he is worthy of the dragon's power?

It was a test, my little Khan, and you passed[3], whispers Sarantuya in his mind. Why does she say this so sadly, he wonders, rather than with the pride he had expected? Or at least some form of respect?

It is not the last such test, little Khan, answers the dragon softly, *and there never will be a last one.*

"So what?" asks Timucin stubbornly[4]. He is overcome[5] with bitterness as he answers his own question. "I understand. It doesn't matter how often I resist the temptation, right? I will always be given another opportunity to fail!" Then he laughs so hard that he even surprises himself. "Is that your idea of fun[6]? Do you dragons enjoy playing cruel[7] games with us humans?"

The figure of Arbesa goes pale and her beautiful face fades into the whiteness. The golden dragon appears in her place. Her razor-sharp[8] claws[9] tear into the jagged rocks[10] under the snow, her teeth flashing[11] and her golden wings whipping[12] through the air. It is as if she can hardly stop herself from tearing him into shreds[13]. Here, watching her, Timucin gets

1 **to unleash the full fury of the dragon** – *die volle Macht des Drachen entfesseln*
2 **to crush** – *zerschmettern*
3 **to pass** – *bestehen*
4 **stubborn** – *störrisch, hartnäckig*
5 **he is overcome with sth** – *ihn überkommt etw.*
6 **Is that your idea of fun** *(Redewendung)* – *Ist das eure Art von Humor?*
7 **cruel** – *grausam*
8 **razor-sharp** – *messerscharf*
9 **claw** – *Kralle*
10 **jagged rocks** – *zerklüftete Felsen*
11 **to flash** – *blitzen*
12 **to whip** – *peitschen*
13 **tearing him into shreds** – *ihn in Stücke zu reißen*

his first real idea of the power of the dragon, a power that can lay waste[1] to whole worlds.

Sarantuya reads his thoughts, just like she reads all of his mind, and her fury[2] subsides[3]. She is deeply sad as she pulls her wings back to her body with a mighty rustle[4] and her claws stop scratching at the rocks.

Well, I'm going to do something that I am not really supposed to do, little Khan, thunders[5] the dragon's voice in his thoughts. *I am going to tell you what is going to happen in the future. Your most difficult challenge is still ahead, and in order to overcome[6] it, you will need to be stronger than you've ever been.*

The dragon's wings start beating again, she straightens up[7], spreading[8] her wings until she covers the skies.

You will have the chance to get Arbesa back, but you will have to pay an extreme price to do so, little Khan. Are you willing[9] to do this?

Of course he is, it doesn't matter what it costs, and he is about to answer just that. But before he can, Sarantuya spreads her outstretched[10] wings even further and, in one sudden move, jumps up into the skies. A golden flash – and she is gone.

DRACHENFRAGE

Which face from his past does Timucin see in a vision?

Timucin searches the skies, then the snow flurries[11] around him. He closes his eyes and listens within himself. But there is nothing. Sarantuya is gone, and he now feels very alone.

1 **to lay waste to** – *verheeren*
2 **fury** *Zorn*
3 **to subside** – *(hier) erlöschen*
4 **rustle** – *Rauschen*
5 **to thunder** – *donnern*
6 **to overcome** – *überwinden*
7 **to straighten up** – *sich aufrichten*
8 **to spread** – *ausbreiten*
9 **willing** – *bereit, willens*
10 **outstretched** – *ausgestreckt*
11 **flurry** – *Gestöber*

The Lonely Warrior

TR. 03

He hurries[1], but night falls before he can reach their improvised campsite[2]. If Chuzir had done as he was told and not lit a fire, Timucin may never have found him[3]. Although his sense of direction[4] is very good, shaped[5] by his life on the steppe, he has trouble finding his way in this empty wasteland[6]. The cold has followed him on his path from the top of the mountain, as well as the darkness which makes every step more dangerous than the last. Nightfall has brought thick, low cloud cover[7] which obscures[8] the moon and stars and fills the air with snow.

The only warrior Timucin has left sits with his knees drawn to his chest[9], wrapped[10] in a blanket at the fire. He turns his back to Timucin as he emerges from the snow like a white ghost. Chuzir neither moves nor says anything as Timucin sits down at the fire. He moves in as close to the crackling[11] fire as he can without burning himself and the two sit for a while in silence. Perhaps each is waiting for the other to say something, or perhaps Chuzir is afraid of being told off[12] by his young khan for having so clearly disobeyed his orders[13] and lit a fire.

Timucin did not give this order for nothing[14]. They haven't seen any sign of the Tajin for almost a week. However, they cannot be sure that

1 **to hurry** – *sich beeilen*
2 **campsite** – *Lager*
3 **Timucin may never have found him** – *Timucin hätte ihn niemals gefunden*
4 **sense of direction** – *Orientierungssinn*
5 **to be shaped by** – *geprägt sein von*
6 **wasteland** – *Ödnis*
7 **low cloud cover** – *schwere, tief hängende Wolken*
8 **to obscure** – *bedecken*
9 **with his knees drawn to his chest** – *mit angezogenen Knien/Beinen*
10 **wrapped** – *gehüllt*
11 **to crackle** – *prasseln*
12 **to be told off** – *gescholten werden*
13 **order** – *Befehl*
14 **for nothing** – *ohne Grund, von ungefähr*

they have shaken their pursuers off[1]. Just a small campfire like this one could well spoil[2] a whole week's effort[3]. But Timucin enjoys its warmth and probably would not have found his way back without the flickering[4] light.

There is perhaps another reason for their silence, however, that Timucin has only just remembered. It was on this very spot[5], at the foot of Burchan Chaldun, that Chuzir betrayed him. Timucin has long forgiven[6] his brother in oath[7], thanks in part to Sarantuya's advice[8]. But he hasn't forgotten. Since their escape together from the Tajin's summer encampment[9], he has not spoken about what happened. Now he begins to understand why Chuzir was so quiet as they moved closer to the mountain. He had seemed to be avoiding[10] Timucin's eye as they walked.

Why don't you tell him? says Sarantuya's silent voice.

Tell him what? replies Timucin silently.

That you have forgiven him, answers the dragon. *Your friend is suffering*[11].

Timucin has asked himself this question at least a dozen[12] times since they started off to this forgotten corner of the world. On the other hand, isn't the fact that they are together and that he has not beaten him to death[13] proof[14] enough that he has forgiven him?

1 **to shake one's pursuers off** – *seine Verfolger abschütteln*
2 **to spoil** – *verhunzen*
3 **effort** – *Anstrengung*
4 **to flicker** – *flackern*
5 **this very spot** – *genau hier*
6 **to forgive sb** – *jdm. verzeihen*
7 **brother in oath** – *Schwurbruder*
8 **advice** – *Rat*
9 **encampment** – *Lager*
10 **he had seemed to be avoiding** – *er schien auszuweichen*
11 **to suffer** – *leiden*
12 **dozen** – *Dutzend*
13 **to beat sb to death** – *jdn. erschlagen*
14 **proof** – *Beweis*

However, he understands what the dragon means. There are some things that need to be talked about, no matter how obvious[1] they may seem. But he isn't quite ready to say that yet.

Instead Timucin says: "We cannot go any further up there."

Chuzir answers with a slight, tired nod[2]. The whole situation breaks Timucin's heart. As easy as it was for him to escape the Tajin and flee from their camp, things only got harder afterwards. Two of the warriors who had accompanied[3] Chuzir died, and the others disappeared one by one. Now he is alone with Chuzir. He knows that Chuzir would follow him anywhere now, even if it means certain death – and not just because of the oath of brotherhood they took all those years ago.

They sit for a while longer in uncomfortable silence[4] until Timucin says: "You know, you don't have to come with me."

Chuzir looks up at him over the flames, and Timucin can see the question in his eyes: *Where are you going?* He remains silent, however, so Timucin adds: "You do not owe[5] me anything else. You don't need to throw your life away because of some silly oath."

Perhaps that isn't quite the right way of saying it, especially to Chuzir, who is not just his brother in oath, but has never forgiven himself for his treachery[6]. Timucin's words must be a slap in the face[7] for him, but nonetheless Timucin continues: "Chuzir, I release[8] you from your oath – you owe me nothing more."

Chuzir shakes his head so strongly that his hood slips[9]. "But I… but I…"

"Yes, you did wrong," interrupts Timucin before he can speak the word that they both never want to hear again, the word that almost de-

1 **obvious** – *selbstverständlich*
2 **slight, tired nod** – *leichtes, müdes Nicken*
3 **to accompany** – *begleiten*
4 **uncomfortable silence** – *bedrücktes Schweigen*
5 **to owe sb sth** – *jdm. etw. schulden*
6 **He has never forgiven himself for his treachery.** – *Er hat sich diesen Verrat nie verziehen.*
7 **slap in the face** – *ein Schlag ins Gesicht*
8 **to release (from oath, bonds)** – *entbinden (von einem Eid, von Fesseln)*
9 **to slip** – *verrutschen*

stroyed their friendship. "You did wrong, but you made up for it[1] when you risked your life to save me from the Tajin camp."

Chuzir is silent, but his face becomes even sadder[2]. Timucin asks himself what he might have said wrong. Chuzir has come this far with him, much further than can be expected[3]. Now there is nothing left for them, except perhaps being recaptured[4] and probably a slow and painful death. It was almost exactly on this spot, five years ago now, that Chuzir betrayed him and brought such terrible misfortune[5] not just to Timucin, but also to his mother and Arbesa. Nevertheless, he has paid dearly[6] for this mistake, and asking him to lay his life down is too much.

Don't you think you should finally explain it to him like that? asks Sarantuya.

Timucin struggles[7] with himself for a moment. It has never been easy for him to forgive. And it is all the more[8] difficult because the mistake was so great. But, he knows that it is the right thing to do. Just as he is opening his mouth to speak, Chuzir suddenly starts[9]. He looks alarmed and tense[10]. Almost without realising that he is doing so[11], Timucin reaches for the sword[12] under his coat. He realises that he is almost incapable of gripping[13] it, because his fingers are so cold.

DRACHENFRAGE

What is the special connection between Chuzir and Timucin?

"Someone is coming," says Chuzir in a loud whisper.

1 **to make up for sth** – *etw. wiedergutmachen*
2 **sadder (sad, sadder, saddest)** – *trauriger (traurig, trauriger, am traurigsten)*
3 **than can be expected** *(Redewendung)* – *als zu erwarten wäre*
4 **to recapture sb** – *jdn. wieder gefangen nehmen*
5 **terrible misfortune** – *großes Unglück*
6 **to pay dearly** – *etw. teuer bezahlen*
7 **to struggle with oneself** – *mit sich ringen*
8 **all the more difficult** – *umso schwerer*
9 **to start** *(hier)* – *zucken, auffahren*
10 **tense** – *angespannt*
11 **almost without realising that he is doing so** – *beinahe ohne sein eigenes Zutun*
12 **sword** – *Schwert*
13 **to grip** – *festhalten*

"And this someone is not an enemy," adds an unseen person, the words almost inaudible[1] over the wind and the fire. Nevertheless, Timucin thinks that he recognises the voice.

"Which is your good fortune[2], by the way[3]. If we were pursuing[4] you, you both would be dead or captured by now. It's amazing you two are still alive with your carelessness[5]. Your fire is visible[6] from miles away and your horses leave trails[7] in the snow that even a blind man could follow."

A masked[8] figure emerges from the snow flurries[9]. The person stands in front of the boys. The fire is between them, so they can see that the person lifts both hands to remove its hood[10]. Timucin recognises the voice as the light of the fire falls on the figure's face – it is Üdschin!

"It pains me to say it[11], but you still have much to learn, my son."

1 **inaudible** – *unhörbar*
2 **to be good fortune** – *pures Glück sein*
3 **by the way** – *nebenbei, beiläufig*
4 **to pursue** – *verfolgen, jagen*
5 **carelessness** – *Unvorsichtigkeit, Nachlässigkeit*
6 **visible** – *sichtbar*
7 **trails** – *Spuren*
8 **masked** – *vermummt*
9 **snow flurries** – *Schneegestöber*
10 **hood** – *Kapuze*
11 **It pains me to say it** *(Redewendung, veraltet) – Ich sage es nur ungern*

Help Arrives

TR. 04

For one, two, perhaps three long heartbeats, Timucin cannot breathe, let alone think clearly. He sits, paralysed[1], staring at his mother as though[2] she were a ghost from his past. In fact, wrapped up[3] in white fabrics[4], she looks more like a phantom than a human. Suddenly, he jumps up and runs to her, marching straight through the fire and throwing up sparks as he does so. He presses his mother so tightly[5] that he almost lifts her off the ground. She stumbles back[6] and is about to fall over, but another figure appears in the snowy darkness and catches her. Through the white flurries, a whole group of ghost-like figures[7] becomes visible and Chuzir starts to shout – his surprised voice shows more fear than happiness, but that doesn't change the situation.

Üdschin is back! His mother, whom he has assumed to be dead[8] for all these years, is here – unharmed[9] and alive. That is all that counts. For some time, they stand in each other's arms, hugging[10] and laughing. It is Üdschin who eventually breaks the embrace[11], softly pushing Timucin back to arm's length and looking at him from head to toe[12]."

"You've grown," she says, "and you've become a real man… well, almost! You're still as brash[13] and careless as ever[14]."

1 **paralysed** - *gelähmt*
2 **as though** - *als ob*
3 **wrapped up** - *eingehüllt*
4 **fabric** - *Stoff*
5 **tight** - *fest*
6 **to stumble back** - *zurückstolpern*
7 **ghost-like figures** - *Schemen*
8 **whom he has assumed to be dead** - *die er für tot gehalten hat*
9 **unharmed** - *unversehrt*
10 **to hug** - *drücken, herzen*
11 **embrace** - *Umarmung*
12 **from head to toe** *(Redewendung)* - *von Kopf bis Fuß*
13 **brash** - *ungestüm*
14 **as ever** - *wie eh und je*

Timucin is still having trouble hearing her, and his thoughts are so confused that he feels a bit dizzy[1]. The others seem to read the confusion in his face and soon Üdschin decides to take the initiative[2], waving to the men behind her. One of them comes forward and stamps[3] out the fire with sparks flying high into the air, revealing the shadows of additional[4] men.

It takes a second for Chuzir to react, jumping up and drawing[5] his sword. The man who had just put out[6] the fire moves so fast that, before Chizur can even realise what is happening, he is lying on his back, disarmed[7] and gasping[8] for air.

"Stop this nonsense[9]," says Üdschin, shaking her head[10]. She sighs[11] more than she shouts, sounding more resigned[12] than angry. The warrior obeys[13] immediately, ramming the sword into the frozen ground just a hand's width[14] away from Chuzir's face and taking a step back.

Chuzir growls[15] angrily and gets up onto his hands and knees, trying to grab his sword as he does so. This time, it is Üdschin who throws him onto his back with a hard slap. Her voice gets louder, but it is still more filled with motherly reproach[16] than with real anger.

1 **dizzy** - *schwindelig*
2 **to take the initiative** - *die Initiative übernehmen*
3 **to stamp out the fire** - *das Feuer austreten*
4 **additional** - *weitere*
5 **to draw a sword** - *Schwert zerren*
6 **to put out** - *löschen*
7 **disarmed** - *entwaffnet*
8 **to gasp** - *japsen*
9 **nonsense** - *Unsinn*
10 **to shake one's head** - *den Kopf schütteln*
11 **to sigh** - *seufzen*
12 **resigned** - *resigniert*
13 **to obey** - *gehorchen*
14 **hand's width** - *Handbreite*
15 **to growl** - *knurren, brummen*
16 **reproach** - *Tadel*

"You should stay down, my lad[1]," she says. "Don't you think you've done enough damage[2] as it is?"

Chuzir is clever enough to actually stay on the ground this time. Although, perhaps he behaves like this due to[3] the fact that another warrior is now standing over him. With the fire dying, Timucin does not really see the warrior's face, but he guesses[4] who it is – even if he cannot believe who he is seeing.

"Ilhan," he murmurs disbelievingly[5] as he recognises the young warrior, his oldest enemy. Timucin can hardly believe it. Ilhan and his father were the ones who betrayed Timucin, his mother and Arbesa – chasing them into the wilderness. Ilhan's father even declared himself khan over Timucin's clan.

"Not just Ilhan," says Üdschin, lifting her hand to stop him from replying. "I know you've got a thousand questions to ask, and I will answer them all, but not now – there are Tajin nearby. I don't know how far away they are, but we've found their tracks. We saw your fire and they may have too, so we must move quickly."

"What… but… but how? How did you get here?" he stammers[6]. "I mean… what?"

His voice trails off[7] and suddenly he finds himself fighting[8] against tears, his feelings threatening to overwhelm him. He hastily[9] drops his gaze[10] so that no one sees the tears in his eyes. After all, he is no longer a boy but almost a man, and the future khan of his clan. This kind of behaviour is really not fitting[11] for a khan.

1 **lad** – *Junge, Bursche*
2 **to do damage** – *Schaden anrichten*
3 **due to** – *wegen*
4 **to guess** – *erahnen*
5 **disbelievingly** – *ungläubig*
6 **to stammer** – *stammeln*
7 **to trail off** – *verstummen*
8 **to fight against sth** – *gegen etw.kämpfen*
9 **hasty** – *hastig*
10 **to drop one's gaze** – *den Blick senken*
11 **to fit** – *angemessen sein, passend sein*

"I looked for you, Timucin," answers his mother, "and I'm sorry it took me so long to find you. Then again, you didn't make it very easy for us to track you."

"But I…" Timucin falls silent in the middle of the sentence as he realises what his mother has just said.

"You looked for us?"

"You are my son, Timucin," replies Üdschin softly. "What kind of mother would I be if I did not do everything possible to save you?"

"I didn't mean that…," he begins, but Üdschin interrupts him.

"Then again, I suppose it was my fault[1] for thinking you were still with the Tajin. I should have known[2] that they could not hold you against your will[3] for very long. You are your father's son after all."

"My Lady," says Ilhan.

"Yes, yes, you are right – there will be time to talk later. Now, we must go before the Tajin really do pick up[4] our tracks," agrees Üdschin.

"But I still have so many questions," says Timucin.

"Not now," says Üdschin, cutting him off with a regal gesture[5] and turning to the men behind her. "Cover[6] our tracks and look for a safe path out of this valley."

Without stopping, she pulls Chuzir's sword from the ground, but does not return it to him, passing it to Ilhan instead. He puts the sword under his coat.

Chuzir's expression[7] grows even darker, but he remains silent. Timucin also keeps his questions to himself, although his burning curiosity[8] makes it difficult. He says nothing until Ilhan and the other men come back. Timucin expects them to return with the horses he and Chuzir have been

1 **I suppose it was my fault** – *Es war wohl meine Schuld*
2 **I should have known** – *ich hätte wissen sollen*
3 **against one's will** – *gegen jdns. Willen*
4 **to pick up** – *aufnehmen*
5 **regal gesture** – *herrische Geste*
6 **to cover** – *verwischen*
7 **expression** – *Miene, Gesichtsausdruck*
8 **burning curiosity** – *brennende Neugier*

riding, but instead they are leading two much healthier-looking animals. His mother reads the question on his face and answers.

"The horses you rode on are exhausted, and if we have to flee quickly, they will almost surely die. You don't want that, do you? Don't worry[1], they will find their way back to us once they have recovered."

Timucin still does not like the idea of leaving the two ponies that have been so faithful[2] to Chuzir and him. His mother may be right, but he feels like he is leaving two friends high and dry[3].

He banishes these thoughts[4], stupid as they are, swinging himself into the saddle[5] with as much force as he can muster[6]. Chuzir hops onto his horse as well and heads over towards Timucin. Üdschin shakes her head, however, and Ilhan grabs hold of his horse's reins[7] and holds him back.

"What is this?" asks Timucin. "Why can Chuzir not ride next to me?"

His mother answers: "He may accompany us until we reach safety, but I will not have him close to me."

"But…"

"Watch him, Ilhan," continues Üdschin. "And if he tries to flee, you know what you must do."

Ilhan answers silently with a nod and pulls immediately on the reins, leading Chuzir's horse away. Timucin turns back to his mother and speaks in an angry tone.

"What is the meaning of this[8]? Chuzir is my friend. I would not be here without him!"

"Yes, that is true," replies his mother sarcastically. "If he had not betrayed us, you would never have been a Tajin slave – would never have been called Khan of the Pigs. Yes, you should be very grateful[9] for this!"

1 **don't worry** – *keine Sorge*
2 **faithful** – *treu*
3 **to leave sb high and dry** – *jdn. im Stich lassen*
4 **to banish a though** *(Redewendung)* – *einen Gedanken verscheuchen*
5 **saddle** – *Sattel*
6 **to muster (force)** – *(seine Kräfte) zusammennehmen*
7 **rein** – *Zügel*
8 **What is the meaning of this?** *(Redewendung, veraltet)* – *Was hat das zu bedeuten?*
9 **grateful** – *dankbar*

"I know that he betrayed us then, but that was a mistake and he knows that now. He is very sorry, and…"

"You still trust him, and I do not understand why," interrupts his mother. "I know he was your friend and your brother in oath. As your mother, I want you to forgive him. But as Lady Khan[1] of our tribe, I cannot allow myself to think like that."

She interrupts herself for a moment as Ilhan returns, bringing with him another horse, which she mounts[2] with agility quite remarkable for her age[3].

"We shall ride back to my clan. When we are there, I shall decide what we do with him."

"What to do with him?" repeats Timucin disbelievingly[4]. Chuzir has always been his most loyal friend – well, mostly. Ilhan, meanwhile, the warrior standing next to his mother, brought disaster[5] to the clan. How has he become Üdschin's most trusted soldier after what he and his father did? Üdschin seems to read these questions in Timucin's eyes and gestures[6] to him to be silent.

"I know what you want to say, my son," she says, "and you are right."

"Oh, am I?" shouts Timucin. "Right about what? About Ilhan's treachery and his father, and…"

"Ilhan's father," says Üdschin, interrupting her son sharply, "was a traitor. He may not be directly responsible[7] for the death of your father and the ruin[8] of our clan, but his actions surely didn't help either. But Ilhan's father is dead now, and those who stood with him too. They have paid for their deeds[9]."

1 **Lady Khan** – *weibl. Khan*
2 **to mount (a horse)** – *aufsitzen*
3 **with agility quite remarkable for her age** – *mit ziemlich bemerkenswerter Geschmeidigkeit für ihr Alter*
4 **disbelieving** – *ungläubig*
5 **disaster** – *Unglück*
6 **to gesture to sb** – *jdm. etw. bedeuten*
7 **to be directly responsible for sth** – *die unmittelbare Schuld an etw. tragen*
8 **ruin** – *(hier) Untergang*
9 **deeds** – *Taten*

"Ilhan is his father's son," replies Timucin angrily, "and he was the worst of them all. How can you trust him now?"

"He did what his father told him to, just like any good son would have," replies Üdschin, "and just like your father would have expected of you."

"He is a traitor," repeats Timucin, "how can you trust him?"

"He made a mistake," grants[1] Üdschin, "an awful mistake with awful consequences, but he has paid for this mistake. He knows he did wrong and has given me his word and begged forgiveness[2]."

"And that makes everything fine?" says Timucin bitterly.

"No," replies his mother, "but being khan means more than just having power, Timucin. It means that you must take responsibility for those who swear allegiance[3] to you. The highest duty of any khan is the duty to forgive, my son. You will need to learn that."

"Oh," hisses[4] Timucin, "and Chuzir's oath to me means less than Ilhan's?"

His mother does not answer and gives him no opportunity[5] to continue. She turns her horse and rides off so fast that he has to make an effort not to fall too far behind. He wonders what she meant when she talked about riding back to "my" clan.

DRACHENFRAGE

According to Üdschin, what is the most important thing a khan has to do?

He has no time to ask the question, though, because at that exact moment, an arrow comes hissing out of the darkness, missing his mother by a hair's breadth[6] and hitting the man behind her.

1 **to grant sb sth** – *(hier) jdm. etw. einräumen*
2 **to beg forgiveness** – *um Vergebung bitten*
3 **to swear allegiance to sb** – *jdm. Treue schwören*
4 **to hiss** – *zischen*
5 **opportunity** – *Gelegenheit*
6 **hair's breadth** – *Haaresbreite*

The Smell of Blood

TR. 05

The battle was as short as it was brutal. Timucin remembers it as a kind of nightmare[1] in which everything appears to happen simultaneously. There were cries and ghostly[2] figures flickering in the snow. There were arrows whizzing past and horses screeching[3] and stamping. He smelled fear, blood and death in the air. After some time, Ilhan stumbles[4] out of the fight.

"My Lady," he gasps, out of breath and panting[5], "are you…"

"Get the others, quickly," interrupts Üdschin, who now looks nothing like[6] the fragile[7] old woman he remembers. "We need to leave now!"

Ilhan nods, but gestures to stop Üdschin storming[8] past him. "The path is blocked," he says. "We have only fought their advance-guard[9] – there are more coming into the valley as we speak."

"How many?" asks Timucin.

"Too many," answers Ilhan, speaking to Üdschin. "We cannot fight them here or we will all perish[10] – you too, my Lady."

"Then we need another way out," decides Üdschin, to which Ilhan only shakes his head.

"I fear that we are trapped[11], my Lady," he replies, "and we shall have to fight."

"Didn't you just say that fighting would mean certain death?" asks Timucin.

1 **nightmare** – *Alptraum*
2 **ghostly** – *geistergleich, schemenhaft*
3 **to screech** – *kreischen*
4 **to stumble** – *stolpern*
5 **to pant** – *keuchen*
6 **to look nothing like** – *etw./jdm. nicht ähnlich sehen, nicht aussehen wie*
7 **fragile** – *gerbrechlich*
8 **to storm** – *stürmen*
9 **advance-guard** – *Vorhut*
10 **We would all perish** *(veraltet)* – *Es wäre unser aller Tod*
11 **trapped** – *eingefangen*

"We just can't fight from here," replies Ilhan, still turned to Üdschin. "We need a better place to defend ourselves."

"There is nothing of the sort[1] here," replies Üdschin.

"Perhaps," counters[2] Timucin. "What about the peak[3]?"

Üdschin looks at him doubtfully. Ilhan seems not to understand and asks: "What peak?"

"The Holy Mountain," answers Timucin. "The peak. We will be safe up there."

"But nobody goes up Burchan Chaldun," protests Ilhan.

"I do," answers Timucin. "I was up there twice. I know the way, and it is so narrow that one man would be able to defend the mountain against an army. Let me show you the way."

Ilhan's expression makes very clear what he thinks of Timucin's suggestion, but Üdschin does not let him reply. She gestures her order and speaks.

"Go and get the others," she says. "Timucin and I shall wait here."

"But, my Lady, nobody goes up Burchan Chaldun – it is forbidden[4]!"

"Well, let's hope that the Tajin see it that way too," answers Üdschin. "Now go! Or would you rather wait until they are all here and then talk to them about their beliefs in this regard?"

This seems to be a clear enough answer for Ilhan. He does not look particularly enthusiastic[5], but after a surly[6] nod, he sets off[7] as fast as he can and Üdschin turns to Timucin, looking grave[8].

"I hope you know what you are doing, my boy," she says. "There is only one path to the peak of the Holy Mountain. If we go up it, we will eventually have to come down the same way." Instead of answering, Timucin asks a question

1 **There is nothing of the sort** – *So etwas gibt es nicht*
2 **to counter** – *widersprechen, erwidern*
3 **peak** – *Gipfel*
4 **forbidden** – *verboten*
5 **enthusiastic** – *begeistert*
6 **surly** – *mürrisch*
7 **to set off** – *aufbrechen, losgehen*
8 **grave** – *ernst*

"Why does he call you 'my Lady'?"

"Because I am his leader," replies Üdschin.

"But that's impossible! No clan has ever taken a woman…"

"… as a leader?" interrupts his mother.

Timucin is also surprised at the tone of voice in which his mother now speaks. She would never have spoken to his father like that, let alone[1] interrupt him.

"No clan has ever been as badly humiliated[2] and betrayed as ours," continues Üdschin.

"But you are a woman," protests Timucin, "and I am…"

"… you are the son of a khan who was betrayed and murdered," interrupts Üdschin once again, no longer bothering to disguise her contempt[3]. "That does not necessarily[4] make you a khan – you need more than just the right father. If you want, we can fight for the title as it was once customary to do[5]."

Timucin can't decide what is more shocking: Üdschin's harsh[6] words or the fact that she actually pulls back her coat and places her hand on the hilt of the dagger[7] in her belt. Then again, he would not have contradicted[8] her in any case. He is too sorry about saying what he has just said that he bites his tongue. He wishes he could take back his words[9].

DRACHENFRAGE

Whose idea is it to retreat to the peak of the Holy Mountain – and why?

1 **let alone** – *geschweige denn*
2 **to humiliate** – *demütigen*
3 **no longer bothering to hide her contempt** – *nun in eindeutig verächtlichem Ton*
4 **necessarily** – *zwangsläufig*
5 **as it was once customary to do** – *wie es früher Sitte war*
6 **harsh** – *hart, forsch*
7 **hilt of the dagger** – *Dolchgriff*
8 **He would not have contradicted her** – *Er hätte ihr nicht widersprochen*
9 **to take back one's words** – *seine Worte zurücknehmen*

"I don't want to hurt[1] you, Timucin," continues Üdschin in a softer[2] tone, "but this is not the right time to have this kind of talk. The men will not do as you say[3]."

"You mean that they won't obey the Khan of the Pigs?" says Timucin.

"No, I mean that they won't follow a boy who they have not seen for years and whose right to be khan is not clear," answers Üdschin calmly[4].

"But I…"

"But what? Do you want to go and talk this through with Ilhan and the others – right in the middle of this battle[5]?"

Talking is about the last thing that Timucin wants to do with Ilhan, even if the battle does appear to be over for now. He can hear a wounded[6] warrior sighing and the sound of horses' hooves[7] disappearing into the distance. Apart from that, the world seems silent.

"No." Timucin finally answers his mother's question in a far meeker[8] voice than he would have liked.

"Well, come on then," says Üdschin, finally lowering her hand from the dagger. She wraps[9] her coat back around herself as though[10] feeling the terrible cold of the snowstorm for the first time.

Ilhan returns with two men, pulling a third, lifeless[11] form[12] between them. For a few moments, Timucin clings[13] to the hope that it is a Tajin warrior, but then he sees it is Chuzir. He seems to have been wounded

1 **to hurt sb** – *jdn. verletzen, jdm. wehtun*
2 **soft** – *sanft*
3 **to do as sb says** – *auf jdn. hören*
4 **calm** – *ruhig, entspannt*
5 **battle** – *Schlacht*
6 **wounded** – *verletzt*
7 **hoof** – *Huf*
8 **meek** – *kleinlaut*
9 **to wrap sth around oneself** – *sich in etw. einwickeln*
10 **as though** – *als ob*
11 **lifeless** – *leblos*
12 **form** – *Form; hier: Gestalt*
13 **to cling to sth** – *sich an etw. festklammern*

in the fight and now hangs, pale and bleeding[1] in the arms of the two warriors.

"Where are the others," asks Üdschin, her eyes filled with rage[2].

"Aktai and Moruje are dead," answers Ilhan. "The others are gathering what little supplies[3] we have left. Most of our horses have bolted[4]."

"Dead?" asks Üdschin. "Both of them?"

"We killed three of them," replies Ilhan proudly. "Only two of them got away[5]. They will think twice about[6] attacking us …"

"Then get the others," interrupts Üdschin. She points to Chuzir: "Leave him here. Timucin and I will look after him."

Timucin kneels down[7] next to Chuzir and feels for his heartbeat. He is alive, but Timucin does not know how badly wounded he is. He runs his fingers[8] over Chuzir's body, searching for the wound. Although he is no healer[9], as a child of the steppe, he has seen plenty of wounds and injuries[10]. Chuzir rolls on his side and pulls his knees to his chest, he is trembling[11] and his face has gone as pale as the snow he is lying in. He is glistening[12] with sweat and completely silent. Timucin's heart stops for a moment as he discovers the deep stab wound in his shoulder. Without hesitating[13], he takes off his coat and uses his dagger to cut off a piece of his shirt to use as an improvised[14] bandage. He tries to tie it around the

1 **to bleed** – *bluten*
2 **rage** – *Zorn*
3 **supplies** – *Vorräte*
4 **to bolt (horses)** – *davonlaufen*
5 **to get away** – *entkommen*
6 **to think twice about doing sth** *(Redewendung) – es sich zweimal überlegen, ob man etw. macht*
7 **to kneel down** – *sich niederknien*
8 **to run one's fingers over sth** – *etw. abtasten*
9 **healer** – *Heilkundiger*
10 **injury** – *Verletzung*
11 **to tremble** – *zittern*
12 **to glisten** – *glänzen*
13 **without hesitating** – *ohne zu zögern*
14 **improvised** – *improvisiert*

wound, but the blood soaks[1] through the rough fabric too quickly for it to be of any use[2].

Chuzir flinches[3] slightly as Timucin applies pressure[4] to the wound. He tries to push Timucin's hand away and Timucin realises that he is probably causing his friend a lot of pain[5]. Feeling helpless, he stands up.

"Do not worry. He will recover[6]," says Üdschin. "You know Chuzir, he is strong."

Timucin hears footsteps[7] behind him, turns around and sees a bent-over[8] figure coming towards them against the strong winds. It is probably Ilhan or one of the other men returning.

He is wrong.

The figure is in fact a Tajin warrior who thinks that he has found his fellows[9] in the misty snow. When he realises who he has found, he growls like an angry dog, draws his sword and leaps[10] at Üdschin. She reacts with superhuman[11] speed, saving herself from otherwise[12] certain death by ducking away from the Tajin's sword. If she had stayed standing, it would have surely taken her head off. Instead, she jumps at the attacker[13] and hits him so hard that he loses his balance[14]. She pulls back and draws her dagger.

Timucin screams piercingly[15], draws his sword and runs at the warrior's back. The Tajin warrior does not even bother[16] to turn and face Timucin,

1 **to soak** - *tränken*
2 **to be of use** - *etw. bewirken, etw. nützen*
3 **to flinch** - *zusammenzucken, zurückzucken*
4 **to apply pressure** - *Druck ausüben*
5 **to cause sb pain** - *jdm. Schmerzen zufügen*
6 **to recover** - *sich erholen*
7 **footsteps** - *Schritte*
8 **bent over** - *gebückt*
9 **fellow** - *Gefährte*
10 **to leap at sb** - *sich auf jdn. stürzen*
11 **superhuman** - *übermenschlich*
12 **otherwise** - *sonst*
13 **attacker** - *Angreifer*
14 **to lose one's balance** - *das Gleichgewicht verlieren*
15 **to scream piercingly** - *gellend schreien*
16 **to not bother to do sth** - *sich nicht die Mühe machen, etw. zu tun, es sich sparen etw. zu tun*

but elbows[1] him so hard in the face that Timucin thinks his head is about to burst. He is in so much pain that he cannot see anything or stand up. He sinks to his knees and his sword slips out of his hands.

He hears Üdschin scream, not just in fear, but in pain. Her cry cuts through the mist like a white-hot blade[2], reaching his numbed[3] senses. He grabs his sword and jumps up – running at the two figures. He aims at the Tajin and stabs[4] with his sword as hard as he can.

He is surprised by how easy it is. The sword stabs through the coat, the leather armour[5] and the body of the attacker with almost no resistance[6], coming out between his shoulder blades[7]. At first, Timucin does not understand why his hands are touching the Tajin warrior's chest, or why the warrior's eyes are suddenly filled with an expression somewhere between surprise and sheer disbelief[8].

As his hands, still clasping[9] the sword, are covered by a warm, sticky[10] liquid, Timucin understands that he has stabbed the warrior. The Tajin falls to his knees so suddenly that Timucin lets go of the sword and jumps back. The warrior takes a long, painful breath and then drops his sword, falling to the side. Timucin's eyes are wide at the horror of the scene.

"Are you injured, my Lady?" shouts a voice from behind them. Ilhan emerges from the dark snow flurries.

"No," replies Üdschin. "Help the boy!"

Ilhan gives Timucin a hateful[11] look before obeying his order and kneeling down next to Chuzir. He roughly pushes away Timucin, who

1 **to elbow sb** – *jdm. mit dem Ellbogen ins Gesicht stoßen*
2 **blade** – *Klinge*
3 **numbed** – *betäubt*
4 **to stab** – *stechen, mit der Klinge stoßen*
5 **leather armour** – *Harnisch*
6 **resistance** – *Widerstand*
7 **shoulder blades** – *Schulterblätter*
8 **sheer disbelief** – *schierer/reiner Unglauben*
9 **to clasp** – *umklammern*
10 **sticky** – *klebrig*
11 **hateful** – *hasserfüllt*

almost falls backwards into the snow. Timucin decides not to shout at Ilhan, saving his angry words for later. He goes to his mother.

Two other men have come with Ilhan, two warriors who Timucin has never seen before.

"What do you think?" Üdschin turns to Ilhan.

"He's lost a lot of blood, but he will survive[1]," answers the warrior. He has bandaged the wound on Chuzir's shoulder and stopped the bleeding. "I don't understand why we are saving this traitor[2]!"

"Because this 'traitor' saved my son's life. Now go and look for the others," orders Üdschin. "Tell them to hurry up!"

The two warriors run off obediently[3]. Üdschin gives Timucin an odd[4] look before turning and going to the dead Tajin. Timucin follows and looks down at the body, as difficult as it is for him. He recognises the man – he was in the Tajin's summer encampment when Timucin was their prisoner[5]. All the Tajin had been cruel to him, and this one more than most others. Timucin thinks he should feel satisfaction[6] at seeing him lying there in his own blood, but he does not. If anything, it feels worse because he knew the man.

"You must take back your sword," says his mother, "for you may well need it again."

Timucin crouches next to the body and reaches for the sword, sticking out of the dead man's chest. Somehow, he can't pull it out. He knows how awful[7] it was to stab the man. The thought of pulling it back out and covering himself in more blood – the same blood now drying on his fingers – is more than he can bear[8]. Instead of his own weapon[9], he takes the dead man's sword and puts it through his belt.

1 **to survive** - *überleben*
2 **traitor** - *Verräter*
3 **obedient** - *gehorsam*
4 **odd** - *sonderbar, seltsam*
5 **Prisoner** - *Gefangener*
6 **satisfaction** - *Zufriedenheit*
7 **awful** - *schrecklich*
8 **to bear** - *ertragen*
9 **weapon** - *Waffe*

"So, how does it feel to have killed a man?" asks Üdschin.

"Kill?" repeats Timucin, shocked. "He wanted to kill you, mother!"

"Yes, and you, and your friend," says Üdschin. "But nonetheless, you have killed him."

"I had no other choice!" protests Timucin, who asks himself why his mother is saying this.

"I know that," she answers calmly, "but this does not change the fact[1] that you have ended a human life."

"But I..., but I..."

"This man," interrupts Üdschin, "may have been our enemy, and you are certainly right that he would have killed us all without a moment's thought[2]. But he too was a man, a son and perhaps a brother. He definitely had parents and may have even had a wife and children that loved him. Somewhere, there will be a family waiting for this man to return – and now he will not. This was the work of your hands, of one movement."

What should I have done, then? he wants to ask, but all he can manage to say[3] is swallowed by a sob[4]. Why is his mother torturing[5] him?

"You had no other choice," continues Üdschin after looking at him for a while in a way he does not understand. "I too would have killed him if I had been able, and anyone else would have too." She shakes her head as he starts to reply. "It is never easy to take another human life, Timucin, and you can never let it become easy. One day, you shall be khan, and you will have to decide the fate[6] of more than just one human life. Don't ever forget what you have learned here."

1 **This does not change the fact that...** – *Das ändert nichts an der Tatsache, dass ...*
2 **without a moment's thought** *(Redewendung)* – *ohne mit der Wimper zu zucken*
3 **to manage to say** – *etw. herausbekommen (Wörter)*
4 **sob** – *Schluchzen*
5 **to torture** – *quälen*
6 **to decide the fate of sth** – *über das Schicksal von etw. entscheiden*

The Secret Girlfriend

TR. 06

What Timucin said about the mountain turns out to be true[1]. The narrow[2] passage up the mountain side is so easy to defend that the group can repel[3] the attackers by simply throwing snowballs. Timucin is too upset[4] about the man he has killed and about his brother in oath to take part in the fight. He is fairly certain that the snowballs his clansmen are throwing are made up of more than just snow. They put stones and other hard objects into them to do more damage. During the night, the Tajin make three attempts[5] to fight their way up the mountain. Timucin can hear the clash[6] of weapons and the cries of battle[7]. The Tajin eventually give up for the night and retire[8] to lick their wounds. Üdschin's warriors are all unharmed. Indeed, the peak of Burchan Chaldun is both holy and completely unconquerable[9], a sort of natural fortress[10]. By the same turn, this makes it a kind of trap[11] from which it is almost impossible to escape.

Timucin spends the whole night next to Chuzir. Ilhan said that he would survive, and Timucin would like nothing more than to believe this, but Chuzir seems to be getting worse and worse. At first, he lies quietly under his blankets, sighing from time to time[12]. As the night goes on, he gets a fever[13]. Soon, he is hallucinating[14], tossing and turning[15] in his

1 **to turn out to be true** - *sich als richtig erweisen*
2 **narrow** - *schmal*
3 **to repel (attackers)** - *zurückschlagen (Angreifer)*
4 **to be upset** - *bestürzt, aufgeregt, traurig sein*
5 **attempt** - *Versuch*
6 **clash** - *Zusammenstoß*
7 **cry of battle** - *Schlachtruf*
8 **to retire** - *(hier) sich zurückziehen*
9 **unconquerable** - *uneinnehmbar*
10 **a sort of natural fortress** - *eine Art natürliche Festung*
11 **trap** - *Falle*
12 **from time to time** - *dann und wann, ab und zu*
13 **fever** - *Fieber*
14 **to hallucinate** - *halluzinieren, fantasieren*
15 **to toss and turn** - *sich hin und her werfen*

sleep so violently[1] that Timucin has no choice but to tie[2] him down for his own good. It breaks his heart to do it.

Chuzir does not get any better until just before dawn[3]. Once Timucin sees that his friend seems to be doing a little better, he tries to get some rest[4]. He sleeps lightly, waking up again after little more than an hour. The only pleasant thing he sees in this moment is his mother's face looking down at him.

"Your friend is being taken care of[5]," answers Üdschin, "so you can continue sleeping." Timucin tries to sit up, until his mother shouts at him. "Do you want to exhaust[6] yourself so much that *he* will have to look after *you*? Do you think he risked his life just so that you can prove to us all what a brave[7] warrior you are?" She answers her own question by shaking her head and pushing him back down.

"Not knowing when to rest is no sign of bravery[8], but rather of stupidity[9]!"

"Now you sound like Sarantuya."

"Saran-who-ya?"

"Err... just someone I, uh... met," answers Timucin evasively[10], "you could call her a friend."

"What do you mean by 'you could call her a friend'?" asks Üdschin, before waving away[11] her own question with her hand and faking[12] a smile. "Never mind, it's none of my business[13]. I did not want to embarrass[14]

1 **violently** – *heftig, gewaltig*
2 **to tie sb down** – *jdn. fesseln*
3 **dawn** – *Morgendämmerung*
4 **rest** – *Ruhe, Erholung*
5 **Your friend is being taken care of.** – *Für deinen Freund ist gesorgt.*
6 **to exhaust oneself** – *sich erschöpfen*
7 **brave, bravery** – *tapfer, Tapferkeit*
8 **bravery** – *Mut, Tapferkeit*
9 **stupidity** – *Dummheit*
10 **evasively** – *ausweichend*
11 **to wave away** – *wegschicken*
12 **to fake sth** – *etw. simulieren*
13 **it's none of my business** – *das ist nicht meine Angelegenheit, das geht mich nichts an*
14 **to embarrass sb** – *jdn. in Verlegenheit bringen*

you." She gets up and rushes off[1], and Timucin uses this moment to sit up and take a look around.

He really is exhausted. He sighs as his head and shoulders fall forward, grits his teeth[2] to stop himself from sighing more and draws[3] his blanket around his shoulders. His face hurts badly, so he carefully feels it with the tips of his fingers. He is in pain, but everything seems to be where it should be, even if it doesn't feel like it used to. He remembers getting elbowed yesterday.

"Don't worry, my brave warrior, it's all still there." His mother is back with a wooden bowl in her hand – there is steam coming out of it[4] and it smells wonderful. She sits down next to him, slowly and gracefully[5], and gives him the bowl. It is so hot that it almost burns his fingers, but the delicious[6] vegetable soup smells so good that he reaches for the wooden spoon and starts to gulp[7] it down.

"Although it doesn't look as bad as it did yesterday," says his mother, "I think your nose is broken. Don't worry though, Sarantuya will like it – I'm sure of that."

Timucin keeps eating and tries to pretend[8] he hasn't heard his mother's comment. This does not work, of course, since Üdschin is not just his khan (which he hasn't quite understood so far), but also his mother – and at this point, she is an extremely curious[9] mother.

"Where did you meet this girlfr… this, uh, person 'that you could call a friend', then?" she asks again. "While you were with the Tajin?"

Timucin sips down another two spoonfuls of soup, which is starting to liven[10] him up a little. Then he does what he should have done right

1 **to rush off** – *davoneilen*
2 **to grit one's teeth** – *die Zähne zusammenbeißen*
3 **to draw** – *ziehen*
4 **There is steam coming out of it** – *Es dampft daraus*
5 **graceful** – *anmutig*
6 **delicious** – *köstlich*
7 **to gulp sth down** – *etw. gierig herunterschlucken*
8 **to pretend** – *so tun, als ob*
9 **extremely curious** – *äußerst neugierig*
10 **To liven sb up** – *jds. Lebensgeister wecken*

away – for even the very gods of Burchan Chaldun are powerless against the burning curiosity of a mother when her son talks about girls who could be girlfriends.

"It's not like you think," he says calmly.

"What do you think I think, then?" asks his mother mischievously[1].

"Sarantuya is not a girl," he answers, "and the only girls of any kind I met with the Tajin were the dogs whose food I stole because it tasted better than the rotten leftovers[2] they gave me." The well-meaning[3] teasing[4] expression on his mother's face disappears.

"I'm sorry, Timucin, I really didn't want to…"

"I only love Arbesa," continues Timucin in a serious tone, "and I only ever have. I will never love another woman like her."

His mother now looks very embarrassed, and although Timucin is almost pleased to have the upper hand[5] for the first time in a while, her expression touches him. He keeps eating, not just because he is hungry, but because it allows him to avoid her gaze.

"Forgive me," she asks, "I didn't mean to hurt you."

"You haven't either," says Timucin, not very convincingly[6]. He curses[7] himself for even mentioning Sarantuya's name. Only Arbesa knows about his secret dragon, and that is the way it must stay.

Because you still don't really believe I exist, I suppose?

Nonsense, thinks Timucin angrily, *what does that have to do with it?*

And you think they will call you mad. A khan who speaks with an invisible dragon who only exists in his mind? Sarantuya's voice has the usual mix of friendly scorn and hidden wisdom[8], as well as gentle[9] sorrow. *It would not be a very good way to win the trust of your future warriors, would it?*

1 **mischievous** – *verschmitzt*
2 **rotten leftovers** – *verfaulte Abfälle*
3 **well-meaning** – *gutmütig, gutgemeint*
4 **teasing** – *neckisch*
5 **to have the upper hand** – *die Oberhand haben*
6 **convincing** – *überzeugend*
7 **to curse oneself** – *sich verfluchen*
8 **wisdom** – *Weisheit*
9 **gentle** – *sachte, sanft,*

It is one of the very few moments when Timucin is really angry with Sarantuya, and his face shows it. His mother notices and looks even more upset[1].

"You still think about her, don't you?" she asks. Timucin nods, without lifting his eyes from the bowl of soup.

"I will find her again," he promises, "no matter what I have to do and how long it takes." Üdschin nods, is silent for a while and then asks: "Why?"

"Why? *Why?*" repeats Timucin, suddenly looking up at her.

"Yes, why?" says his mother again. "I know what you'll say: Arbesa is your future wife. She was promised to you when you were children, and perhaps you think that it is your noble duty[2] to save the woman who was chosen to be your wife as khan?"

"That has nothing to do with it…!" says Timucin, before his mother interrupts him again.

"She is not your wife, my son. She may well have been promised[3] to you, but you two never actually became man and wife. Well, unless you two…"

"… no!" shouts Timucin so loud that he surprises himself and his mother seems to feel forced[4] to smile. He feels his cheeks[5] turning red with embarrassment. Üdschin becomes more serious again and speaks in a gentle tone of voice.

"It wouldn't make any difference in any case. I like Arbesa, you know that. She's a lovely girl and I would have liked nothing more than for her to be[6] my daughter at your side. But the gods have chosen another path

DRACHENFRAGE

Why is Timucin so embarrassed about having mentioned Sarantuya?

1 **upset** – *betroffen*
2 **noble duty** – *edle Pflicht*
3 **She may well have been promised** – *Sie mag dir versprochen worden sein*
4 **to feel forced to do sth** – *sich zu etw.genötigt fühlen*
5 **cheek** – *Wange*
6 **I would have liked nothing more than for her to be…** – *Nichts hätte mein Herz mehr erfreut als dass sie … gewesen wäre*

for us." On this, Timucin stops eating his soup – it sticks in his throat[1]. He looks straight into his mother's eyes.

"What do you mean by that?[2]"

"She was your bride, my son, but never your wife," answers Üdschin. "As such, you have no obligation to her[3]. Nobody expects you to risk your life to save her. And why should you?"

"Why?" groans[4] Timucin. "Why?! Are you being serious?"

The look in Üdschin's eyes answers this question for him. It is now getting more and more difficult for Timucin to keep his cool[5]. Anger is welling up[6] inside of him.

"It's not just about me, my son," continues Üdschin, "not even about you."

"It's about Arbesa," agrees[7] Timucin with a shaky[8] voice. "I know."

"And you know what happened to her, don't you?"

At this, Timucin's heart starts to beat faster. Now he is convinced that his mother just wants to torture him, for whatever reason. After all, he knows just as well as his mother what happened to Arbesa – he too was there on that horrible day. According to what Chuzir told him, although the Tajin took her prisoner, they sold her to the Merkites. Since the Merkites are friends of Timucin's clan, they must have treated[9] her well. They may well have returned her to her powerful father, head of the strong and wealthy Voshon clan.

"You've been asking yourself since that day why you chose me, why you gave me the extra horse to flee, while leaving your bride to be captured. You don't know, do you? But I know why." Üdschin grabs for[10] his

1 **to stick in one's throat** – *jdn. wurmen*
2 **What do you mean by that?** – *Was soll denn das heißen?*
3 **to have an obligation** – *eine Verpflichtung haben*
4 **to groan** – *ächzen*
5 **to keep one's cool** – *die Ruhe bewahren*
6 **anger is welling up** – *Wut kocht hoch*
7 **to agree with sb** – *jdm. zustimmen*
8 **shaky** – *bebend*
9 **to treat sb well** – *jdn. gut behandeln*
10 **to grab for sth** – *nach etw.greifen*

hand, but he pulls it away and her eyes darken[1]. Her voice sounds sad but convinced as she continues.

"You had to choose between us: an old woman who they would have probably killed on the spot and your bride, the daughter of a khan who would have perhaps paid a ransom[2] for her. So you chose to save one life for sure[3] and perhaps a second, rather than to sacrifice[4] one with certainty and risk a second."

"That's not the way it was," he protests, hot tears in his eyes. He does not try and stop them, for her words are truer than he is ready to admit.

"No, Timucin – that is how it was. It's just that the decision was not made by a boy in love, but by a future khan – the one inside you, waiting to get out. It was the right decision."

"It was wrong," he cries, "I should never have done it[5]! I should have..."

What? asks a voice in his thoughts, a voice that could be either his own or Sarantuya's. *What? Give Arbesa the horse and let my mother die a certain death?* No, he really couldn't say that.

"In that case, it will be the future khan, not the boy in love, who frees her," he answers defiantly[6]. He expects another scornful answer or a reproof[7] of some kind, but Üdschin just shakes her head.

"You cannot, my son, for perhaps that boy in love would have gone looking for her, even if he did die doing it, but the future khan of the Kijat clan will not.

"Oh really," snaps[8] Timucin, "and why is that?"

"Because they sold her into slavery. The khan of the Tajin clan kept her for his personal amusement[9]. A little while later, he sold her to a

1 **to darken** – *verfinstern, sich trüben*
2 **ransom** – *Lösegeld*
3 **for sure** – *ganz sicher, bestimmt*
4 **to sacrifice** – *opfern*
5 **I should never have done it.** – *Ich hätte das nicht tun dürfen.*
6 **defiant** – *trotzig*
7 **reproof** – *Verweis*
8 **to snap**- *(hier) fauchen*
9 **amusement** – *Vergnügen*

barbarian tribe[1] in the North. I somehow doubt she will have had it any better with them."

Timucin stares[2] at her with his eyes wide open. It is as if his heart has stood still.

"How…? I thought… I thought she had been sold to the Merkites! She would have been safe there. Her father could have bought her back. Did he not…?"

"What? Pay a ransom for her?" interrupts his mother, shaking her head in answer to her own rhetorical[3] question: "No. I'm sure Chuzir did not mean to lie to you – they did want to sell her to the Merkites. He couldn't know that it would be different in the end."

"But… but she is the daughter of the Voshon khan, and the Voshon are rich!"

"She is his daughter, but he is the khan, and as such he cannot pay a ransom for a daughter who has been dishonoured[4] by his enemies. That's why the Merkites were not interested in her either. He can no more pay a ransom for her than you can take her as a wife – the men would not follow you!"

"Then I shall go for her alone," says Timucin. His mother is about to interrupt, but now it is his turn to stop her from speaking. "I shall find and free her, and I shall do so no matter whom I must fight. I love her!"

"Love," says his mother, followed by a strange noise which he does not quite understand, "love is a big word, Timucin. You would have to give up everything for it. None of the men would ever recognise you as leader[5] ever again."

"Leader of what?" he asks, bitterly. "The Kijat clan is no more."

"Yes, these are bad times, my son," agrees Üdschin. "Many are dead and the others are scattered to the four winds[6]. But some of the men still

1 **Barbarian tribe** – *Barbarenstamm*
2 **to stare at sb** – *jdn. anstarren*
3 **rhetorical** – *rhetorisch*
4 **to dishonour** – *entehren*
5 **leader** – *Anführer*
6 **scattered to the four winds** – *in alle Winde zerstreut*

follow me, and things will change for the better. One day, our clan will come together again and it will need a leader – a strong khan to guard[1] it and help it flourish[2], not an old woman." She pauses for a second. "You could be that khan, my son. Do you want to give up[3] all of that for some girl – a girl who may not even want you anymore?"

"Yes," answers Timucin without a moment's hesitation – and he means it.

1 **to guard** – *hüten*
2 **to flourish** – *gedeihen*
3 **to give sth up** – *auf etw. verzichten*

The Traitor

TR. 07

Timucin is surprised at how easily he manages to sleep after this emotional[1] talk. He falls into a very deep slumber[2] and only wakes up again around midday. His body is as exhausted as it was before and his face still hurts (and not just around his nose). Nevertheless, he feels slightly rested[3]. After standing up and rubbing his sleepy eyes, he goes to Chuzir. The men have been considerate[4] enough to put him next to a rock out of the wind, but they have left him on the bare ground[5]. The only blanket they have left him is the snow that has fallen on him in the last few hours. His face is so white that Timucin is afraid for a moment that his brother in oath has died from his wounds.

As he approaches Chuzir, his brother does not open his eyes. Instead, he slowly and painfully pushes himself into a sitting position, his back resting on the rock behind him. He tries to smile and greets Timucin: "My Khan."

Timucin sits down next to him cross-legged[6] and looks at him carefully before answering. He is deeply worried because, although he is relieved[7] to find Chuzir alive and conscious[8], his brother in oath is not well. His face is almost the same colour as the snow he is lying in. His cheeks look grey and there are deep, almost black shadows under his eyes. He is trembling under the thin cloak the men gave him in the night.

"You look half-dead," says Timucin, "even if you are doing better. I suppose it is good that you are in a mood for jokes[9] – even if they aren't very good."

1 **emotional** – *aufwühlend*
2 **slumber** – *Schlummer*
3 **rested** – *ausgeruht*
4 **considerate** – *rücksichtsvoll*
5 **bare ground** – *nackter Boden*
6 **to sit cross-legged** – *im Schneidersitz sitzen*
7 **relieved** – *beruhigt, erleichtert*
8 **conscious** – *bewusst*
9 **In a mood for jokes** – *zu Scherzen aufgelegt*

"What do you mean?"

"Chuzir, I am not your khan anymore," answers Timucin bitterly, "you heard Ilhan."

"Ilhan may well have grown up since we last saw him, but that has clearly not made him any cleverer. If anything, he has grown more stupid with age," replies Chuzir. "You will always be my khan."

"That is good to hear," says Timucin, "because that means we can start our own clan, even if it isn't very big." Chuzir nods at this suggestion as if he is taking it seriously, and Timucin starts to wonder if they have not, in fact, just founded[1] a new clan. "And although we will never be the biggest clan in the world, we can at least be the smallest!"

Timucin forces himself to laugh at his own joke, even if he is not at all in the mood to do so. His face darkens with anger as Chuzir tries to make a movement and he sees that his hands are tied.

"Why are your hands still tied up[2]?" Chuzir answers with a shrug of the shoulders, a shrug which he seems almost immediately to regret[3], judging by the expression of pain on his face[4].

"Perhaps they are still afraid of me. After all, I still have one healthy arm that might be dangerous," answers Chuzir, making a joke despite the pain. Timucin does not manage to laugh this time, though.

"How is your shoulder doing?" he asks.

"It's still there," answers Chuzir, "even if I can't say that I'm happy about that at the moment. From now on, I shall have more respect for injured soldiers. It really hurts!"

Timucin draws his dagger and bends towards Chuzir in order to cut through his bonds[5]. He is almost finished when he hears heavy steps behind him and Ilhan's booming voice.

1 **to found** – *gründen*
2 **tied up** – *zusammengebunden*
3 **to regret sth** – *etw. bedauern*
4 **judging by the expression of pain on his face** – *dem Ausdruck von Schmerz auf seinem Gesicht nach zu urteilen*
5 **bonds** – *Fesseln*

"What are you doing, you stupid boy? Who told you to release the prisoner?"

Stupid boy? That's a new one[1]. Timucin has been intending[2] to speak to Ilhan at some point to clear a few things up, but now he realises that he had better do it sooner than later[3]. If it goes on like this[4], it will only get more difficult to tell Ilhan who is boss[5].

He stands up very slowly and turns around, without sheathing[6] his dagger.

"Nobody," he says, "but who can stop me?"

Ilhan pushes out his bottom lip[7] and stamps through the snow towards him like a furious ox. It has been almost six months since he last saw Ilhan. Back then, he was a powerful boy, at least a hand bigger than Timucin. He must have stopped growing before Timucin, though, because he is now a bit shorter than him, but he is still much stronger. His eyes smoulder[8] with rage, and Timucin would not have been surprised if he had started hitting him. Instead, he comes right up to Timucin and stops, which is perhaps a mistake – now he has to look up to Timucin to speak to him.

"He stays tied up. I don't trust him," says Ilhan.

"Are you afraid that he's going to beat you up[9] with his one good arm, then?" asks Timucin sardonically[10].

"He is a traitor, why should we trust him?"

1 **That's a new one.** – *Das ist neu.*
2 **to intend to do sth** – *sich etw. fest vornehmen*
3 **that he had better do it sooner than later** – *dass er es besser früher als später machen muss*
4 **if it goes on like this** – *wenn es so weiter geht*
5 **to tell sb who is boss** – *jdn. in seine Schranken weisen*
6 **to sheath** – *einstecken*
7 **to push out the bottom lip** – *Unterlippe vorschieben*
8 **to smoulder** – *lodern*
9 **to beat up** – *verprügeln*
10 **sardonic** – *höhnisch, hämisch*

"He can't even walk," replies Timucin. "Don't make a fool out of yourself[1]!"

"He stays tied up!" insists[2] Ilhan. "Either you tie him back up, or…"

"Or what?" asks Timucin, smiling[3].

Ilhan's hand falls to the hilt of his sword. He looks at the dagger in Timucin's hand, then at his face, and then back to the weapon. Timucin can see his mind working[4], but before he can say anything, several figures come towards them and Üdschin shouts:

"Enough! What is this nonsense? Have you both gone mad?"

Ilhan's hand drops from his sword and Timucin lowers[5] the dagger, although he does not sheath it.

"What is going on here?" asks Üdschin.

"I was cutting Chuzir's bonds because they are hurting him," answers Timucin. "Ilhan did not seem to agree with me doing it."

"Is that the truth?" asks Üdschin.

"We can't trust him," answers Ilhan defiantly. "He will disappear as soon as he can and betray us to the Tajin."

"Oh yes, clearly. I suppose he will slip down into the valley unseen[6] and tell them that we are up here," replies Timucin scornfully. Ilhan starts to jump at him, but Üdschin gestures to both of them to be still.

"Enough!" she cries. "If you've got this much energy left over[7], then save[8] it to fight the Tajin. She pauses for a moment, gives Chuzir a thorough once-over[9] and then, as if she has answered a question in her own mind, speaks.

1 **to make a fool out of oneself** – *sich lächerlich machen*
2 **to insist** – *beharren*
3 **smiling** – *lächelnd*
4 **He can see his mind working.** – *Er kann sehen, wie es hinter seiner Stirn arbeitet.*
5 **to lower** – *sinken lassen, senken*
6 **to slip unseen** – *schleichen*
7 **to have energy left over** – *überschüssige Kräfte haben*
8 **to save sth** – *sparen*
9 **to give sb a thorough once-over** – *jdn. prüfend/durchdringend ansehen*

"Timucin is right," she says. "There is no need to torture him, we are better than that."

"But he…" says Ilhan, starting to object[1], but Üdschin speaks to him so sharply[2] that he winces[3] as if he has just been whipped.

"Do you understand me, Ilhan?!"

In reply, his face goes blank. He nods, murmurs[4] something that only he understands and walks away as fast as he can. Üdschin's eyes follow him, more worried than angry. But the anger returns as soon as she turns round to face Timucin.

"I am disappointed in you," she says. "Do you really think this is the right time for a childish spat[5]?"

"It is all my fault, my Lady," says Chuzir. "I was the one who…"

"Follow me!" says Üdschin, ignoring Chuzir and storming off[6].

TR. 08

Timucin runs after and only catches her as she stands on the edge of the mountain and can go no further.

"Why are you so angry with me?" he asks. "I didn't do anything!"

Üdschin does not answer immediately, but looks down at the country beyond[7] Burchan Chaldun, now bathed in sunlight[8] and seemingly so close that they could reach out and grab it – but it is far out of their reach[9]. There is no way down to this tempting new world. After a while, she sighs deeply and turns round to him, her expression is exhausted.

"I thought you understood what I was trying to tell you this morning."

"But…"

1 **to object** – *protestieren, Einwände erheben*
2 **sharp** – *scharf*
3 **to wince** – *zusammenzucken*
4 **to murmur** – *murmeln*
5 **childish spat** – *kindischer Kampf*
6 **to storm off** – *davonstürmen*
7 **beyond** – *jenseits*
8 **bathed in light** – *lichtdurchflutet*
9 **far out of one's reach** – *unerreichbar fern*

"… you were right, Timucin," she continues. "Everything you said was true. But this isn't about you and your friend. You may well have already been dead without him, but as a khan, you cannot allow that to influence[1] your decision."

Timucin understands what she means very clearly, but he is silent. If that is what being a khan is about, then he is not at all sure that he wants to be a khan anymore.

"You and Ilhan will never be good friends, that is clear, but you should try to gain his respect."

"Should I fight him, then?" he asks stubbornly.

"You would lose," answers his mother quietly, "and even if you didn't, he would fear you, but not respect you. There is a difference between the two. The times when it was always the strongest warriors who became khan is long past[2] – and it is for the better[3]."

"So what should I do to get his respect then?" asks Timucin, not at all sure what his mother is trying to get at[4].

Üdschin is about to answer, but then she shrugs her shoulders[5] and smiles, embarrassed.

"Ilhan is a bad example of what I mean," she admits, turning round and pointing to the men gathered round the fire at the other end of the plateau, trying to keep warm. Timucin does not know any of them, but then[6] he only knows three of the clan following Üdschin – including[7] Ilhan.

"These men owe me nothing, Timucin," she says. "They have no reason to respect me, obey me or be loyal[8] to me – and nonetheless two of them have just died and the others do not know whether they will ever

---

1 **to influence** – *beeinflussen*
2 **long past** – *lange vorbei*
3 **It is for the better.** *(Redewendung) – Es ist auch besser so.*
4 **to try to get at sth** – *auf etw. hinauswollen*
5 **to shrug one's shoulders** – *die Achseln zucken, die Schultern heben*
6 **but then** – *aber schließlich*
7 **including** – *einschließlich, mitgerechnet*
8 **loyal** – *treu*

leave this place alive. Each of them knew the risks when I asked them to follow me, but not one of them hesitated at all. Do you know why?"

As she expects, Timucin shakes his head. On this, Üdschin points back to the men around the fire, and to the two bodies lying across the plateau, wrapped in their cloaks. Timucin realises that they have brought the dead men up the mountain with them, and this is a thought which comforts[1] him.

"They follow me because their khan trusts me," says Üdschin. "They know that they can trust him to make a decision, because he would never decide to do something that might harm[2] the clan."

"Who are they?" asks Timucin.

"Men from the Merkites," answers his mother. "That is the clan of my parents – the clan into which I was born."

"But my father…"

"… stole[3] me from them, yes, many years ago," says Üdschin, interrupting him as has become her habit[4]. "They still speak of this kidnapping[5] in the Merkite yurts today."

This confuses Timucin.

"But didn't you once tell me that it almost caused a war between the Kijat and the Merkites?"

"Yes, it almost did. But they respected your father and after he was murdered[6] and our clan scattered, they took me and the other survivors into their camps. Their khan even sent out search parties[7] looking for you and gave me ten men to help free you. Even if that turned out not be necessary[8]," she adds, smiling briefly[9] and sadly.

1 **to comfort sb** – *jdn. beruhigen, trösten*
2 **to harm sb** – *jdm. schaden*
3 **to steal, stole, stolen** – *stehlen*
4 **habit** – *Angewohnheit*
5 **kidnapping** – *Entführung*
6 **to murder** – *ermorden*
7 **search parties** – *Suchtrupp*
8 **necessary** – *nötig*
9 **brief** – *flüchtig*

"Why are you telling me this?" asks Timucin. *Is it just to make me feel even worse?*

"So that you can understand what it means to be a khan," answers Üdschin. "All of these men have entrusted[1] their lives to me on the word of their leader. These are men who have families, wives and children waiting for them. Do you think they would have done this if they were *afraid* of their khan?" Timucin is still not sure if he understands why his mother is telling him this.

"No," he replies.

"No, they wouldn't have at all," says Üdschin. "I'm an old woman, Timucin, with only a few summers left until the gods call me, and I would like nothing more than to see you lead our clan like your father once did."

"What, from the tents of the Merkite clan?" he counters. Üdschin smiles, as if he has just said something amusing.

"You really are your father's son – he was just like you, you know?"

"How?"

"He too used to act[2] first and think later." She shakes her head lightly to stop him asking another question and then continues to speak: "The Merkite khan is a very generous[3] man, but I cannot ask him to fight the Tajin on my behalf[4]. Once we have survived this, we shall go back to them for the winter, but then we will have to leave. There are not many of us left, Timucin, a handful of warriors and their families, but they need a khan."

"So why don't you ask Ilhan?" asks Timucin, who regrets these words even while he is saying them[5].

1 **to entrust sth to sb** – *jdm. etw. anvertrauen*
2 **to act** – *handeln*
3 **generous** – *großzügig*
4 **on my behalf** – *meinetwegen, in meinem Auftrag*
5 **He regrets these words even while he is saying them.** – *Er bedauert diese Worte schon, bevor er sie ganz ausgesprochen hat.*

"He is still young, Timucin, barely a year older than you, don't forget that. He is just as impetuous[1] as you were – and still are."

"No, he's an idiot," replies Timucin.

"Yes, yes he is," says Üdschin, "but idiots can be right sometimes."

"Right about what?" asks Timucin sceptically[2].

"It took me five years to find you," says Üdschin, "and it wasn't a secret at all that we left to free you. Isn't it strange that Chuzir turned up to free you just a short time before we did?"

Now, although Timucin knows that it wasn't that easy, he can't deny that Üdschin's idea is possible. Nevertheless, he shakes his head.

"He did not come alone. When I met him, he had men with him."

"Did you know them?"

"No," answers Timucin.

"So where are they now?" asks Üdschin.

"Most of them fled once they realised that the Tajin were hunting us," admits Timucin.

"Men without honour," says Üdschin, "men who are not welcome anywhere. We caught one and he told us where you were going. That's the only way we could find you."

"What is so wrong about that?" asks Timucin.

"Well, he told us more," continues Üdschin, "that they had been sent to kidnap[3] you."

"What is the point of all this?" asks Timucin, who does not want to hear what Üdschin is saying.

"I am still a wealthy[4] woman, Timucin," she answers, "but the Tajin never asked for a ransom. They knew that I would never do business[5] with the people who murdered my husband. But I might well have paid someone else to get you back."

Might well? Timucin is hurt.

1 **impetuous** – *ungestüm*
2 **sceptical** – *misstrauisch, skeptisch*
3 **to kidnap** – *entführen*
4 **wealthy** – *vermögend*
5 **to do business** – *Geschäfte machen*

"I do ask myself, though, why your brother in oath did not come to me. Everyone knew where I had fled to."

"Well, maybe he didn't come to you because you think he is a traitor?"

"Isn't he a traitor?"

"No," answers Timucin decidedly[1]. "He did make a mistake that almost cost me my life – that much is true. I hated him for that, for every single minute that I was a prisoner of the Tajin – that is true too. But that is all over now. I know that he regrets the mistake he made and that he will never do it again. I trust him."

DRACHENFRAGE
Where do Üdschin's fighting men come from and why do they follow her?

Üdschin looks at him at length[2] and with a very grave[3] look in her eye: "I hope you are right, my son," she says, "because if not…"

Suddenly, they are interrupted by loud voices from the other end of the plateau. Timucin and his mother both turn expecting[4] to see a horde[5] of armed Tajin storming through the pass[6]. The excitement is coming from another spot on the peak, away from the only way onto it. The men have gathered[7] and are gesticulating and shouting wildly. Timucin sees Ilhan in the middle of the confusion, swinging his sword.

Timucin and Üdschin hurry to the group, as does everyone else on the plateau. The confusion grows and Üdschin has to shout loudly to calm everybody.

"What is going on here?" she yells[8]. "Ilhan, tell me!"

Ilhan turns around so fast that Timucin and several others start. His eyes are black with rage and his voice is trembling.

1 **decidedly** – *entschieden*
2 **at length** – *lange*
3 **grave** – *ernst*
4 **expecting to** – *darauf gefasst*
5 **horde** – *Horde*
6 **pass** – *Hohlweg, Bergpass*
7 **to gather** – *sich zusammentun, versammeln*
8 **to yell** – *schreien, brüllen*

"He's gone!" he hisses.

"Who?" asks Timucin, as if he doesn't know.

"Your friend," answers Ilhan, "your brother in oath, the one who we can all trust with our lives, right? That's why he takes the first opportunity to disappear off to his friends down there!"

"Chuzir has fled?" That does not make any sense! In the night that has just past Chuzir was so ill that Timucin wondered if he would make it through to dawn. And now he has fled? In his condition? And fled to where? There is nowhere to go.

"Perhaps he was afraid that he might have an accident[1] of some kind," responds Timucin angrily.

"An accident?" repeats Ilhan. "Yes, that is tempting[2], I have to say."

"Stop it, you two!" shouts Üdschin. "How did this happen? Did you not assign[3] somebody to guard him?"

"Why would I?" asks the young warrior petulantly[4]. "Timucin was so convinced that he was harmless."

"We will talk about this later. For now, I want him found. He can't have gone far in his condition!"

1 **accident** – *Unfall*
2 **tempting** – *verführerisch*
3 **to assign sb to sth** – *jdn. zu etw. abstellen, jdm. etw. übertragen*
4 **petulant** – *patzig*

The Shadow

TR. 09

Chuzir is nowhere to be found. Ilhan spends the days that follow on the mountaintop looking daggers[1] at Timucin. The Tajin try to take the peak several times, but it is easy enough to repel their attacks. Nevertheless, the situation on the mountain is getting more and more desperate. The group is running out[2] of supplies and firewood[3]. In this biting cold, they will freeze to death without fire.

Every night since he first met her, Sarantuya comes to Timucin in his dreams. She usually comes alone. In one dream, though, he saw her together with Tselmeg, Arbesa's own invisible dragon mentor[4]. Timucin has often thought about how lonely Sarantuya's existence must be, despite all her incredible powers. But these past few nights, she comes with a pale, blurred[5] figure from the mountain fogs. At the start of each dream he can't see who the figure is, but it is definitely a person. Timucin's heart starts to beat faster. Something about these dreams is different – and it is not just because Sarantuya is not alone. He feels that danger is approaching, slowly but surely[6].

Sarantuya? he asks silently.

No one answers. The dragon simply roars, a roar of such anger that Timucin cowers[7] in fear. He shouts her name once and then again, but there is no answer. The second figure that has appeared with Sarantuya starts to become clear. Timucin is both relieved and scared at the same time. He is relieved that the figure is not Arbesa, sent to say goodbye to him. But he is scared because the figure is the Tajin warrior he killed in the valley. His skin is thin and grey like old parchment[8], his eyes are emp-

1 **to look daggers at sb** – *jdm. mit Blicken durchbohren*
2 **to run out** – *ausgehen*
3 **firewood** – *Brennholz*
4 **mentor** – *Berater, Mentor*
5 **blurred** – *verschwommen*
6 **slowly but surely** – *ebenso langsam wie unaufhaltsam*
7 **to cower in fear** – *sich vor Furcht krümmen*
8 **parchment** – *Pergament*

ty of all life, and the blood on his shirt has dried black[1]. There are more ghosts behind him and Timucin thinks that he can make out distorted[2] faces and outstretched hands trying to reach the warrior. Timucin tries to escape these visions, but he cannot. The warrior moves towards him slowly, and the ghosts follow. Timucin understands that the figures behind him are the warrior's loved ones, those who have lost him and have now come to the realm[3] of the dead and damned to search for him.

You killed him, whisper the voices, *you have taken our father, our brother, our husband.*

Their hands reach for Timucin. As they get closer, the hands curl to fists[4] to hit him and claws to scratch him. The dead warrior comes closer and closer, he raises the sword in his hand, preparing to strike Timucin. Suddenly, the blade disappears, but Timucin cannot stop himself from screaming in horror. The warrior keeps following him, and Timucin is gripped by fear[5]. He draws his sword to keep the warrior away from him[6], but the shadows stay where they are. He hears accusing[7] whispers and begins to panic. Without thinking about what he is doing, he stabs with his sword. The blade slips through the grey shadows as easily as it had pierced the flesh of the warrior he killed. As the blade stabs, he hears countless[8] screams: He hears the mothers, daughters and wives from whom he has taken this man, but the warrior is gone. The grey shade lightens and he can see Sarantuya again. She is bigger, more imposing[9] and more awe-inspiring[10] than ever, towering above him in a threatening way. Her scales have gone black, the dead warrior is on her back, but with Timucin's face.

1 **dried black** – *schwarz geronnen*
2 **distorted** – *verzerrt*
3 **realm** (*veraltet*) – *Reich*
4 **to curl to a fist** – *sich zu einer Faust ballen*
5 **to be gripped by fear** – *von Angst gepackt werden*
6 **to keep sth away from oneself** – *sich etw. vom Leib zu halten*
7 **accusing** – *anklagend*
8 **countless** – *zahllos*
9 **imposing** – *imposant, beeindruckend*
10 **awe-inspiring** – *furchteinflößend*

Sarantuya, what is the meaning of this? asks Timucin.

Instead of answering, the dragon turns around slowly, pushing off from the cliff edge and spreading her gigantic[1] wings. She soars[2] into the skies, and the land beyond Burchan Chaldun is changed. The dragon's shadow burns the summery[3], green forests and the lush pastures[4]. In an instant, all of it is dry and barren[5]. The land starts to smoke and the smell of death is on the air. Instead of crystal-clear waters and summer flowers of all colours, armies[6] now march and make the earth shake. The black forces roll[7] across the landscape, laying waste to whatever comes into their path[8]. Fire and war harrow[9] the country and the dragon is still in fury. Wherever its shadow touches the ground, all life is destroyed. War and famine[10] follow in its path.

Suddenly Timucin wakes up. His heart is beating so fast that he can hardly breathe. Although he is lying under two blankets and has his warm cloak on, his whole body is trembling with cold. He knows he has had nothing more than a bad nightmare, but it takes him several moments to find his way back to reality. His mother is sitting next to him, saying something that he does not understand. She seems to be repeating it. Some of the men are looking in his direction.

"Is everything alright?"

At least Timucin is now able to understand Üdschin's question, but he is not able reply to it. He is still half in the dream until she touches his shoulder. He sits up and manages[11] to nod.

1 **gigantic** – *riesig*
2 **to soar** – *emporragen*
3 **summery** – *sommerlich*
4 **lush pasture** – *saftiges Weideland*
5 **barren** – *öde*
6 **army** – *Armee*
7 **to roll** – *(hier) sich wälzen*
8 **laying waste to whatever comes in their path** – *sie zerstören alles, was in ihren Weg gerät*
9 **to harrow** *(veraltet)* – *verheeren*
10 **famine** – *Hungersnot*
11 **to manage to do sth** – *etw. zustande bringen, es schaffen, etw. zu machen*

"Did I… scream?" he asks with a voice so hoarse[1] that he answers his own question.

"You had a nightmare," says his mother. Although she doesn't add "again", Timucin can see it in her eyes. Dreams have been haunting[2] him since they have been up here, and it is getting worse every time. It has never been as bad as this. It isn't just the dead man that frightens[3] him, but the expression in Sarantuya's eyes, which are usually so soft. Her gaze has become so piercing[4] that she can see through his very bones.

He is afraid that the others will see his true feelings, so he pretends to have the shivers[5]. He slides[6] himself towards the fire, now burning so low that it does not help much. The flames are more embers[7] than anything else now, and so weak that they offer almost no warmth. In fact, they seem to make everyone colder. They all know that there are no supplies left. They ran out of food on the third day, now there is only enough wood for a small fire during the night to stop them from freezing to death.

As he carefully takes his hands from under the blanket and holds them over the dying fire, he wonders whether it really was right to bring them all up here. Everybody is suffering from the cold, and Timucin doubts[8] whether the men will really be able to defend themselves if the Tajin change their tactics and try to take[9] the peak again. Perhaps this fire is not saving their lives, but prolonging[10] their deaths.

"Try to sleep a little more," suggest his mother. "There are a few hours left until sunrise."

1 **hoarse** – *heiser*
2 **to haunt sb** – *jdn. heimsuchen*
3 **to frighten** – *erschrecken, ängstigen*
4 **piercing gaze** – *durchdringender Blick*
5 **to have the shivers** – *frösteln*
6 **to slide** – *rutschen*
7 **embers** – *Glut*
8 **to doubt sth** – *etw. bezweifeln*
9 **to take** – *(hier) erobern, stürmen*
10 **to prolong sth** – *verlängern*

Timucin is actually so tired that his eyes are falling closed. Then again, the idea of going to sleep and facing the dead man again is too much. He shakes his head.

"I'm not tired," he says, "and I don't need much sleep."

"Well, we others do," complains one of the men, demonstratively[1] pulling his blanket over his head. Timucin looks sheepish[2] and his mother is barely able to suppress a smile[3]. She goes back to the place she has chosen to sleep, protected[4] from the wind. Timucin gets up and goes to the other end of the plateau that is the highest point of the sacred mountain. The darkness of the night makes it difficult to see where the plateau ends and where the abyss begins. The last few steps he takes are dangerous, but Timucin has walked to this point so often in the last few days and nights that he could reach it with his eyes closed. The fact that the night is so dark that he cannot see his hand in front of his face does not stop him from seeing the land below him. He sees it so clearly as if it were bathed in the midday sun[5]. It has changed now, though, and the fertile soil[6] has become a black morass[7], pounded[8] by countless hooves[9] and laid waste[10] by war and famine. The peaceful future he has imagined for him and his tribe has disappeared into this black desert.

"Why are you showing me this?" he whispers. The wind whispers back, carrying the silent answer of the dragon: *Because it is the way you have chosen, little Khan. The way that I can take you*[11] *if you choose it.*

"But I have never wanted this!" He wonders if he is actually awake or still in the awful dream.

1 **demonstratively** – *demonstrativ*
2 **to look sheepish** – *ein schuldbewusstes/verlegenes Gesicht machen*
3 **to suppress a smile** – *sich ein Lächeln verkneifen*
4 **protected** – *geschützt*
5 **as if it were bathed in the midday sun** – *als wäre es in das Licht der Mittagssonne getaucht*
6 **fertile soil** – *fruchtbarer Boden*
7 **morass** – *Morast*
8 **to pound** – *(hier) zertrampeln*
9 **countless hooves** – *zahllose Hufe*
10 **to lay waste** – *zerstören, verwüsten*
11 **the way that I can take you** – *den Weg, den ich dir eröffnen kann*

It is the way of the dragon. It is the way which you have long since chosen in the depths of your mind.

"I have not chosen it[1]!" protests Timucin, "I have never…"

It is the way of the khan. One day, you will be called Genghis[2], the Khan of all Khans. The world will tremble when your name is mentioned, and people will still whisper it in fear a thousand years later.

He has never wanted this! The dragon has already offered him her power (and warned him of using it). He didn't take it then – why should he take it now?

You will take it because all people do in the end, answers Sarantuya. *The power of the dragon is boundless[3], and what human can resist[4] the call of boundless power?*

"I can!" says Timucin, with deep conviction[5]. "I can resist it. I don't want it!"

"What do you not want?" asks a voice behind him.

It isn't Sarantuya's voice, but he recognises it. Rather than turning around immediately, he counts to five in his mind, time enough to prepare himself. Then he turns around, sending a few small stones flying down the cliff. Timucin has trouble not smiling spitefully[6] as he sees Ilhan start at this sound and take a step back.

"Why are you not sleeping?" he asks instead of answering Ilhan's question.

"I've tried," replies Ilhan, "but somebody was shouting too loudly. Then, once that was over, somebody else started talking to himself[7]. Say, have you got an imaginary friend[8] out there who is coming to save us?"

1 **I have not chosen it. (choose, chose, chosen)** – *Ich habe es nicht gewählt.*
2 **Genghis** – *gemeint ist hier Dschingis Khan. Auf Englisch kann er wie im Deutschen mit dsch am Anfang oder mit g gesprochen werden.*
3 **boundless** – *grenzenlos*
4 **resist** – *widerstehen*
5 **with deep conviction** – *tief überzeugt*
6 **spiteful** – *schadenfroh, gehässig*
7 **to talk to oneself** – *Selbstgespräche führen*
8 **imaginary friend** – *unsichtbarer Freund*

DRACHENFRAGE

What is Sarantuya trying to show Timucin in the nightmare he has?

Timucin is close to telling[1] him the truth, but of course he doesn't. Not just because Ilhan would not believe him, but also because he is worried that the warrior will think him mad[2].

"And it's too cold to get back to sleep[3], anyway," continues Ilhan once he realises that he won't get an answer from Timucin.

"Why don't we go and gather some firewood," suggests Timucin.

Ilhan's answer is a nasty[4] look. Most of the scant[5] bushes and trees on the plateau had been felled[6] by the end of the first day. Since then, their fires have swallowed most of what was left on the ground. They had no choice but to send men back down through the pass to fetch more wood. Such activity does not escape the notice[7] of the Tajin, of course. One of the men they sent did not return from his mission – another three have been lucky to return alive. They are severely wounded. Each piece of wood they brought back has been paid for in blood[8].

"Oh, of course, you'd love that, wouldn't you?" scoffs Ilhan. "Let me guess – I go first and you keep your eyes open and shout if there's a trap?"

The very idea is so absurd that Timucin does not even try to answer. He starts to walk past Ilhan – or tries to. Ilhan puts out his hand and holds him in such an iron[9] grip that Timucin almost cries in pain.

"Not so fast, Khan of the Pigs," he says.

1 **he is close to telling** – *er ist kurz davor, es zu sagen*
2 **to think sb mad** – *jdn. für verrückt halten*
3 **to get back to sleep** – *wieder einschlafen*
4 **nasty** – *gemein*
5 **scant** – *spärlich*
6 **to fell** – *fällen*
7 **to escape sb's notice** – *jdm. verborgen bleiben*
8 **Each piece of wood they brought back has been paid for in blood.** – *Jedes Stück Holz, das sie mitgebracht haben, wurde mit Blut bezahlt.*
9 **iron** – *Eisen, eisern*

Timucin stares at him and forgets to struggle[1]. He hasn't been called that since he escaped the Tajin.

"What's the matter?" asks Ilhan. "Didn't think I'd remember? Only six months ago, we were all calling you that."

Timucin frees himself and tries to go past Ilhan again, but Ilhan steps in his way again. He is smirking[2], his eyes glint viciously[3]. Timucin notices that he is bearing a sword, and that his hand is on the hilt – as if by chance[4].

"Get out of my way," says Timucin quietly.

"Or what?" asks Ilhan.

Timucin is clever enough to say nothing. Ilhan frowns[5] and looks away, and as Timucin follows his gaze, he sees his mother sitting bolt upright[6] on her bedding[7], looking in their direction.

"Of course," says Ilhan sarcastically[8], "your mother. But don't think this is over, Khan of the Pigs. Your mother will not always be waiting to hide you beneath her skirts."

Timucin feels anger welling up[9] inside him. His hand slides under his cloak, but he finds nothing more than the rough cord[10] he is wearing instead of a belt.

"What? Have you forgotten your sword, Khan of the Pigs?" says Ilhan scornfully. "Perhaps I should give you mine. I don't need it."

It's up to you, little Khan.

Why not? Why have the power of the dragon if he is not willing to use it?

1 **to struggle** – *kämpfen, sich abmühen, ringen*
2 **to smirk** – *feixen*
3 **vicious** – *bösartig*
4 **as if by chance** – *als wäre es Zufall*
5 **to frown** – *die Stirn runzeln*
6 **bolt upright** – *hoch aufgerichtet*
7 **bedding** – *Bettzeug, Schlafplatz*
8 **sarcastic** – *sarkastisch, abfällig*
9 **to well up** – *aufwallen*
10 **cord** – *Strick*

Ilhan smirks[1] more and more shamelessly[2], pushes back his cloak and draws his sword in order to offer Timucin the hilt.

"I really do not need it, my Khan. Not to fight with someone as…"

Sarantuya!

Silently and invisibly, the dragon spreads her wings and Timucin feels her power flowing into him. He doesn't grow claws or wings[3], nor does his skin turn into impenetrable[4] armour[5]. In fact, if anything, the change is in Ilhan, who stands with his sword, challenging Timucin, when suddenly the scornful glow in his eyes goes out.

"What… but what…?" he murmurs.

"Sheath your sword," says Timucin, "and find an axe. We are going to fetch some wood."

1 **to smirk** – *grinsen*
2 **shameless** – *unverschämt*
3 **He doesn't grow claws or wings.** – *Ihm wachsen keine Klauen oder Schwingen.*
4 **impenetrable** – *undurchdringlich*
5 **armour** – *Panzer, Harnisch, Rüstung*

The Fight

TR. 10

Ilhan could not find an axe, but Timucin has taken his sword. Üdschin calls for two other men to join them, and the party[1] sets off. For the first part of the way, they don't run into any Tajin. Ilhan pushes his way to the front and leads them down through the pass with his sword drawn. Every now and then[2], he stops and listens, but the only thing they hear is the sound of their own hearts beating and their feet grinding[3] the snow and ice. Even the wind has gone still – as if nature herself is holding her breath.

The worst moment is when Ilhan steps on a dry branch[4]. It snaps loudly, cracking like a whip[5] and everyone freezes instantly. Timucin holds his breath and waits for a dozen Tajin warriors to come running out of the darkness, or at least to hear a shout of warning. But nothing happens. The night is as quiet as it was before. After a few moments, even Ilhan starts to breathe again and lowers his sword.

"Onwards[6]," he whispers, "and be careful!"

He of all people[7]. One of the men murmurs something that Ilhan decides not to hear[8], and they set off more carefully than ever. They reach the bottom[9] of the pass without anything happening, but then Ilhan stops again. Timucin, too, closes his eyes and uses his dragon senses to listen and feel. They must be alone though, for if the Tajin have left watchmen[10] here, then they are not breathing.

"There is something wrong here," murmurs Ilhan.

1 **party** – *(hier) Gruppe, Truppe*
2 **every now and then** – *ab und zu*
3 **to grind** – *(hier) knirschen*
4 **branch** – *Ast*
5 **like a whip** – *wie eine Peitsche*
6 **onwards** – *weiter (voran)*
7 **he of all people** – *ausgerechnet er*
8 **to decide not to hear** – *vorziehen, etw. nicht zu hören*
9 **bottom** – *(hier) Talsohle*
10 **watchmen** – *Wachmänner*

Timucin does not bother to congratulate[1] Ilhan on this clever deduction[2], but steps next to him and gives orders to the others: "Gather wood. Gather as much as you can find, but don't make any noise. Ilhan and I will go on and see what we can find."

If Ilhan has a problem with this order, he hides it in the dark. He sheathes his sword, puts his round shield[3] on his back and waits for Timucin to lead.

The uncanny[4] silence holds. Apart from the sounds that they make marching through the dark forest, there is no other sound at all. The woods are silent. Once they reach the bottom of the Holy Mountain, they discover that the Tajin camp has been deserted[5]. Here and there, the last embers of a fire are visible, but there is no sign[6] of the Tajin. Dark circles in the snow show where their yurts have stood, and just next to the encampment there is a pit[7] for rubbish. Ilhan immediately begins to look through it for anything edible[8].

Timucin knows how Ilhan feels. His stomach is rumbling[9] so loudly that, if the Tajin were still there, they would be able to find them by following the noise. He follows the wide track that they have left behind – it isn't hard. There were a lot of Tajin, it would seem, far more than they had feared, and they haven't made much of an effort[10] to cover their tracks, which lead west out of the valley. Timucin follows their tracks to the end of the long valley and then returns to find Ilhan.

1 **to congratulate sb** – *jdn. beglückwünschen*
2 **deduction** – *Schlussfolgerung*
3 **shield** – *der Schild*
4 **uncanny** – *unheimlich*
5 **to desert sth** – *etw. verlassen*
6 **no sign of sth** – *keine Spur von etw.*
7 **pit** – *Grube*
8 **edible** – *essbar*
9 **to rumble (stomach)** – *knurren*
10 **they haven't made much of an effort** *(Redewendung) – sie haben sich keine besondere Mühe gegeben*

The young warrior has stopped looking through the rubbish left behind by their pursuers. To Timucin's relief[1], he is not chewing[2] on anything unidentifiable[3] either.

"Did you find them?" he says as Timucin approaches.

"They are gone," answers Timucin, "and, from the way it looks, I'd say that they were in a hurry[4].

"You mean that they fled?"

"Well, they are not here in any case," replies Timucin.

"Then perhaps we should use this opportunity to leave here too," suggests Ilhan, "because they may well be back soon."

That is the least of Timucin's worries[5] right now. Judging[6] by their trails, there were at least three dozen warriors – almost a small army. With growing disquiet[7], he asks himself what kind of danger could have scared them so much that they left in such haste[8].

The two warriors have clearly not obeyed Timucin's orders, but have kept close to[9] Ilhan, wondering if the Tajin have really left. They step up[10].

"Go back and get the others," orders Ilhan, "and do it quickly! Tell them to bring only what they need and that they must hurry! We do not know if the Tajin will return!"

The two Merkites disappear back into the darkness so quickly that Timucin is not at all sure if they have understood Ilhan clearly. He looks at Ilhan for a moment and shakes his head.

1 **to his relief** – *zu seiner Erleichterung*
2 **to chew** – *kauen*
3 **unidentifiable** – *unidentifizierbar*
4 **to be in a hurry** – *es eilig haben*
5 **It is the least of his worries.** *(Redewendung) – Das war seine geringste Sorge.*
6 **judging by sth** – *etw. nach zu schließen*
7 **disquiet** – *Unbehagen*
8 **haste** – *Hast, Eile*
9 **to keep close to sb** – *an jdm. dranbleiben*
10 **They step up.** – *Sie treten zu ihm.*

"Are you dissatisfied[1] with the order I gave, oh my Khan?" he asks scornfully. "Would you rather wait here for them to come back? I'm sorry I haven't let that happen."

"Please stop it," sighs Timucin. "We are alone. Nobody can see or hear us, so if you want to say something to me, please just say it."

"I wouldn't know what to say, oh great Khan," replies Ilhan curtly[2]. Timucin is so angry that he has to stop himself from shouting at Ilhan so loud that they will hear them on top of the mountain.

"That is exactly what I mean," he says, controlling himself[3].

"What? What do you mean, my Khan?" counters Ilhan. Timucin notices a look on his face that means that he would rather have said more[4], but did not dare[5].

"You're afraid that my mother will make me khan, aren't you?" asks Timucin. "You think that it should be you, don't you? You think that you should lead our clan – or what's left of it!"

"And what if that is true?" says Ilhan defiantly, avoiding Timucin's gaze. Of course he wants to be khan, but perhaps he is remembering what he saw in Timucin's eyes on the mountain a few moments ago, remembering the fear he suddenly felt.

"Well, if it is true," answers Timucin, "you are getting worried about nothing[6]. I do not want to become khan – not like this!"

Ilhan keeps staring at him, and Timucin is almost completely convinced that he will not get any answer at all. Then Ilhan, suspicious[7], asks a question.

"What do you mean 'like this'?"

"I mean that I do not want to become khan just because I am my father's eldest son."

---

1 **Are you dissatisfied with...?** – *Missfällt dir...?*
2 **curt** – *spröde, schroff*
3 **to control oneself** – *sich (mühsam) beherrschen*
4 **He would rather have said more** – *Er hätte lieber mehr gesagt*
5 **to dare** – *wagen*
6 **to get worried about nothing** *(Redewendung)* – *sich umsonst Sorgen machen*
7 **suspicious** – *misstrauisch*

"But that is the way it is, and it has been so for as long as the world has existed," answers Ilhan.

"Then perhaps it is time for us to change that," says Timucin. "I do not want you to follow me because of some old custom[1]. You are right Ilhan, I do want to be khan someday. If I'm honest, there is nothing more I want in the whole world than to lead the survivors[2] of our clan to the lands on the other side of this mountain, to a country where a new future and a better life awaits[3] us. But I do not want to lead them there because I am my father's son and because this is the custom. They must follow me because they trust me."

"And why should they trust you?" asks Ilhan dismissively[4].

"Perhaps because he is the best person to do it?"

The voice belongs to Timucin's mother. Wrapped in a blanket that is much too thin for the cold, she steps out of the trees behind them. The look in her eyes makes it clear to both of them that she has been standing there for some time and has heard every word. Ilhan bows[5] to her in a manner which seems to lack[6] real respect.

"Why, my Lady, how…?"

"How did you get here?" interrupts Timucin.

"You didn't think I would just sit there with my hands in my lap[7] while my son risks his life, do you? What kind of a mother would I be?"

This isn't exactly what Timucin wants to hear right now. Ilhan's eyes glow with undisguised[8] spite[9], but this glow is soon put out as Üdschin turns round and flashes[10] her eyes at him.

1 **custom** – *Sitte*
2 **survivor** – *Überlebender*
3 **to await sb** *(veraltet)* – *auf jdn. warten*
4 **dismissive** – *abfällig*
5 **to bow to sb** – *sich vor jdm. beugen*
6 **to lack sth** – *an etw. mangeln*
7 **lap** – *Schoß*
8 **undisguised** – *unverhohlen*
9 **spite** – *Schadenfreude, Gehässigkeit*
10 **to flash one's eyes at sb** – *jdn. anfunkeln*

"Ilhan, tell me, how many of our family would follow you as khan? What do you think?"

"I don't know what…" he sputters[1], but Üdschin interrupts him again.

"Yes, you don't know anything, do you? Now, get up there and see that our men make it off of that mountain. After that you can see if the Tajin have left anything of use[2] behind.

Ilhan does not dare to contradict her, but his nod and his facial expression are disrespectful[3] and show defiance if anything.

"And send some men to track the Tajin," adds Üdschin. "We must know where they are riding to."

"I shall take care of that personally, my Lady," says Ilhan. Without waiting for an answer, he turns on his heal[4] and disappears into the darkness. Üdschin silently watches him go, her face shows concern and worry. Then she turns to Timucin.

DRACHENFRAGE

Why do the Tajin not attack them as they leave the mountain?

"He will cause you a great many[5] difficulties, my son," she sighs. "I heard what you said to him."

"And I meant it, too," says Timucin.

"They were wise words," she sighs, "but are you sure that they were clever?"

He is not sure of that at all. In fact, he knows Ilhan well enough to understand that he will simply interpret[6] these words as a sign of weakness[7]. He is silent.

"Even if I don't mean this the way it might sound," continues Üdschin as she realises that Timucin is not going to answer her, "Ilhan is right about one thing: I will not always be there to protect[8] you."

1 **to sputter** – *stottern*
2 **of use** – *von Nutzen*
3 **disrespectful** – *respektlos, verächtlich*
4 **to turn on one's heal** – *auf dem Absatz herumfahren*
5 **a great many** – *sehr viele*
6 **to interpret sth** – *etw. auslegen, deuten*
7 **a sign of weakness** – *ein Zeichen von Schwäche*
8 **to protect sb** – *jdn. schützen*

If anyone else said anything like this, Timucin would be angry, but he understands what his mother is trying to say to him. He also knows that she is wrong and that she has no reason to worry. The power of the dragon means that he has nothing to fear from challengers[1], especially not from young warriors such as Ilhan. There is nobody he has to fear, for Sarantuya has shown him his future, and it is a future of glory[2], the future of a warrior whose name people will still whisper nervously in a thousand years' time. It is a future that he is not sure he wants.

1 **challengers** – *Herausforderer*
2 **glory** – *Ruhm, Glanz*

The Way of the Warrior

TR. 11

For a while, it looks like fate is being kind to them. Not only do all of the men and their animals make it down from the mountain, but the Tajin have left so hastily that several days of food can be found where they had camped. Ilhan, too, has good news when he returns: The Tajin seem to be in a hurry and are not slowing their pace[1] at all. As soon as day breaks, they move out[2]. For the first time in more than a week, they are not afraid that each step they take will be their last. This feeling, however, is soon gone.

With all of the men and their horses exhausted, they make slow progress[3]. Even before the sun reaches[4] its highest point, they are being followed again. Ilhan points in the direction they have come from and Timucin turns his head and follows Ilhan's finger. He has to blink[5] a few times before his tired eyes actually recognise anything, but then he sees what Ilhan has seen. Behind them, a good way back, a group of black dots is dancing in the air. A flock of birds[6] has been forced to fly. Around them, the air starts to darken. In summer, this would be dust created by horse hooves. In this cold winter landscape, it is probably snow, but the cause[7] must be the same.

"We are being tracked," says Ilhan. He is almost whispering so that only Üdschin and Timucin will hear his words. With all his conspicuous[8] behaviour, he could spare himself the effort, thinks Timucin. "It could be the Tajin," adds Ilhan. Üdschin nods, but her face shows her doubt.

"It could be," she answers, "or it could be what made the Tajin flee so fast."

1 **to slow one's pace** – *langsamer werden*
2 **to move out** – *aufbrechen*
3 **to make progress** – *vorankommen*
4 **to reach** – *erreichen*
5 **to blink** – *blinzeln*
6 **flock of birds** – *Vogelschwarm*
7 **cause** – *Grund, Anlass*
8 **conspicuous** – *auffällig*

Timucin wants to say something, but Üdschin shakes her head and continues.

"It doesn't matter who it is. We must be alert[1]. Just because they are the enemies of our enemies, that doesn't make them our friends."

She looks around for a moment and then points in the opposite direction to their pursuers, to a point which looks to Timucin like any other place.

"We'll hide there in those rocks on the hill. We can defend ourselves well there."

Timucin knows that she is clutching at straws[2]. Anyone following them cannot help but[3] see their tracks, and they are far too tired to defend themselves against anyone. Then again, they can't just keep riding, hoping to outrun them. They try to make their exhausted animals run faster to reach the rocky hill in the distance before their pursuers catch up with them. The horses, however, cannot and will not go faster. One falls and breaks its leg. Its rider is lucky[4] to escape with a few grazes[5]. Once they reach the rock-covered[6] hill, they see that the wavy[7] darkness on the horizon has become a clear, dark line. This soon becomes a series of individual shapes. It is impossible to tell just how many riders are headed towards[8] them, but Timucin knows that they are hopelessly[9] outnumbered[10]. Just the thought of trying to fight is ridiculous[11].

Despite this, however, the men prepare as quickly and precisely as he expects men of his tribe to, including Ilhan. Two of the men are so badly wounded that Üdschin sends them off to guard the horses. At least they

1 **to be alert** – *auf der Hut sein*
2 **She is clutching at straws.** *(Redewendung) – Das ist nur ein frommer Wunsch.*
3 **They cannot help but do sth** *(Redewendung) – Sie können es nicht umhin etw. zu tun*
4 **to be lucky** – *Glück haben*
5 **graze** – *(hier) Schramme*
6 **rock-covered** – *mit Steinen bedeckt*
7 **wavy** – *hügelig*
8 **to head towards sth** – *auf dem Weg sein zu*
9 **hopeless** – *hoffnungslos*
10 **outnumbered** – *unterlegen (Zahl)*
11 **ridiculous** – *lächerlich*

feel like they are doing something useful. The other men take up posts[1] in the gaps between the icy rocks and search for cover[2] in the thin bushes. Timucin starts to lose his courage[3] as he takes up his place between the defenders, pulling his bow and quiver[4] from his back. His fingers are frozen stiff[5], so much so that it hurts to lay an arrow on the bowstring[6]. None of the other men are in a better condition than him. If these really are Tajin warriors and they really do attack, then this will be perhaps the shortest and bloodiest defeat these lands have ever seen.

That is the way of the warrior, my Khan. It is the way that you have chosen. Sarantuya's voice has changed since the last time he heard it. It sounds colder and more powerful, but also more sad. Has he really chosen this way, though? Has it not been forced upon him[7]?

"Get ready," orders Üdschin, "and aim low so that they cannot use their shields."

About a dozen arrows are now drawn on bowstrings, held by freezing fingers. Timucin looks towards the wall of horse and armour galloping towards them, and then at the faces of his men. All of the faces are the same: grey, thin, gaunt[8], marked with exhaustion and pain. But none of the faces[9] show any fear. Many of the men look tired to death. Many of their eyes are filled with sadness that this should be their end. But there is no fear, nobody trying to escape their fate, no anger[10]. The men are Merkites, not even part of his clan, but they are ready to die for them at this cold, unknown place. Just because their khan expects it of them.

That too is the way of the warrior, my Khan.

1 **to take up posts** – *sich postieren*
2 **to search for cover** – *Schutz suchen*
3 **courage** – *Mut*
4 **bow and quiver** – *Bogen und Köcher*
5 **frozen stiff** – *steif gefroren*
6 **arrow, bowstring** – *Pfeil, Sehne*
7 **to force sth on sb** – *jdm. etw. aufzwingen*
8 **gaunt** – *eingefallen*
9 **none of the faces** – *keines der Gesichter*
10 **anger** – *Wut, Zorn*

Now, he cannot just hear Sarantuya, but thinks he can see her too, in his mind's eye[1]. She seems different: no longer the soft and gentle giant with golden scales and protective[2] wings, she reminds him of the dragon in his dream, the dark monster whose shadow scorches[3] the earth and brings danger and misery[4] to men.

"No," he says.

Ilhan blinks and looks at him blankly[5]. His mother too stares at him as if to ask: *What do you mean, no?*

Timucin stands up, lowers his bow and then draws his sword, which he also lays on the icy rocks behind him. Their pursuers are now so close that the sound of their thundering[6] hooves on the frozen ground almost drowns him out[7]. He speaks up.

"I do not want this. They are here for me, not for anyone else. I shall go to them."

"You are talking rubbish, my son," says Üdschin angrily. "Now pick up your bow!"

"Or go and protect the horses," adds Ilhan, whom[8] Timucin ignores.

"They are here for me and me alone," he continues decidedly[9], "and I do not want them to join the other three who have already died. I do not want more bloodshed[10]."

"Timucin," says his mother angrily, "do as you are told…"

But Timucin steps out from behind the rock and walks down the flat slope[11]. His mother shouts to him, and a few of the men begin to murmur too, but soon the hammering of hooves, the clang[12] of weapons

1 **In his mind's eye** – *(Redewendung) vor seinem inneren Auge*
2 **protective** – *behütsam*
3 **to scorch** – *verbrennen, versengen*
4 **misery** – *Elend, Not*
5 **to look at sb blankly** – *jdn. verständnislos anblicken*
6 **thundering** – *donnernd*
7 **to drown sb out** – *jdns. Stimme übertonen*
8 **whom** – *den*
9 **decided** – *entschlossen*
10 **bloodshed** – *Sterben, Blutvergießen*
11 **flat slope** – *flacher Hugel*
12 **clang** – *klirren, klingen*

and the crack of heavy leather armour are too loud for their voices to be heard. His heart beats almost as loudly as the army approaches. He has to summon up all of his courage[1] not to turn and run, but he stands as the horses thunder towards him. Just when it looks as if they will ride him down[2], the horses split left and right and surround him. The riders hold their horses and suddenly Timucin is in the middle of a circle of horsemen.

Sarantuya, he thinks desperately, *help me! Give me the power to defeat*[3] *them!*

That is not the way it works, little Khan, whispers the dragon deep in his thoughts, *for I cannot turn your skin into iron and your breath into fire. You know that.*

Of course he does. Sarantuya cannot give him this kind of power. In this moment he feels more afraid for his life[4] than he ever has. The people of the steppe are no strangers to death. He has always thought that death is nothing more than a part of life and never was bothered[5] by the idea of death before. Now he realises that death does not scare him, but dying[6] does.

One of the riders has his horse take a step towards him. The animal snorts nervously and scrapes[7] its hoof in the snow. Timucin tries to recognise the face of the rider. Perhaps it is somebody he knows from the Tajin summer encampment – but he has never seen this man's face before. He has a dark, full beard[8] and black, pitiless[9] eyes. He looks at the other faces, each of them unknown. The Tajin are a large clan with many families, so perhaps they have taken reinforcements[10] from another

1 **to summon up** – *all sein Mut zusammennehmen*
2 **to ride sb down** – *jdn. niedertrampeln*
3 **to defeat** – *besiegen*
4 **part of life** – *Teil des Lebens*
5 **to be bothered by** – *sich Gedanken machen um*
6 **to die, dying** – *sterben*
7 **to scrape** – *scharren*
8 **beard** – *Bart*
9 **pitiless** – *gnadenlos*
10 **reinforcements** – *Verstärkung*

camp. This would explain their sheer number – he is surrounded by at least fifty horsemen.

"Is that the boy?" asks as rough voice.

"Well, he is not one of ours," answers the bearded rider. His dark eyes examine[1] Timucin so closely that it sends a chill down his spine[2]. He realises that he is dealing with the leader, perhaps with the khan of the Tajin himself, so he forces himself to look him in the eyes.

"I am the one you are looking for," he says, his voice not quite as strong as he would like. Somehow, though, he is no longer trembling in fear – well, not much.

"I know that you are hunting me," he says after a silence in which none of the riders speak and the bearded one turns his head from side to side, sizing him up[3]. He is looking at him like some kind of exotic insect that could be either harmless or quite dangerous.

"I give up!" says Timucin.

"Oh, you do, do you?" replies the bearded rider, visibly amused.

"Take me and do what you want with me," adds Timucin, "but leave my men. They have nothing to do with this, they only came to help me. I know that men in your clan have died and that you want blood to pay for blood, but we too have lost good men. We are even[4]. Let the others go and take me."

"Judging by this nonsense, this must be the boy."

"Yes, perhaps the cold and the hunger have driven him mad," says the bearded rider.

"This is a matter that is between us," says Timucin, "and you outnumber[5] me. What honour[6] would it bring upon the Tajin to butcher[7] a handful of exhausted men and an old woman?"

1 **to examine** – *unter die Lupe nehmen, prüfen, untersuchen*
2 **It sends a chill down his spine** *(Redewendung)* – *ihm läuft ein kalter Schauer über den Rücken*
3 **to size sb up** – *jdn. mit den Augen messen, jdn. mustern*
4 **we are even** – *wir sind quitt*
5 **to outnumber** – *in der Überzahl sein*
6 **honour** – *Ehre*
7 **to butcher** – *niedermetzeln*

"The Tajin, my son, are a people[1] without honour who would enjoy such carnage[2]," says his mother from somewhere behind the horses. The bearded rider turns and sees Üdschin approaching, her head held high. The riders make way[3] for her.

"Those were brave words, my son, words worthy of a khan. I only fear that they are misplaced[4] here and would not have helped much if these men really were Tajin."

DRACHENFRAGE

Who does Timucin think the horsemen are as he lays down his weapons?

Timucin does not understand the meaning of what his mother is saying. The bearded rider jumps down from his horse and runs to his mother, hugging her tightly to him. Timucin is surprised beyond all measure[5].

"Üdschin! Thank the gods that you are still alive! I was afraid that we might have come too late!"

Üdschin looks for a moment at what Timucin still thinks are Tajin warriors and then slowly releases herself from the embrace of the bearded rider. She keeps hold of his hand.

"Well, it takes more than just a pack of Tajin to catch me," she says with a wink[6], "but I must admit that I am very happy to see you, Udugur."

She lets his hand fall and beckons to Timucin[7].

"Timucin, this is Udugur, Lord of the Merkites and my father's brother."

1 **a people** – *ein Volk*
2 **carnage** – *Gemetzel*
3 **to make way for sb** – *jdm. den Weg freigeben*
4 **misplaced** – *fehl am Platz*
5 **beyond all measure** – *maßlos*
6 **with a wink** – *augenzwinkernd*
7 **to beckon sb to oneself** – *jdn. zu sich winken*

The Decision

TR. 12

"Merkites," repeats Timucin, "Lord of the Merkites?"

"Yes, and you can count yourself lucky[1], my boy," says Udugur with a nod. "If we had been the Tajin you thought we were, you would have been dead[2] by now."

"Merkites?" asks Timucin again. "You mean, you're not Tajin?"

"You didn't tell me that your son was deaf[3], Üdschin," says Udugur scornfully.

"But… how…?" sputters Timucin. "How… how did you get here? Why did you come?"

"That is a good question," says Üdschin, supporting her son.

"We had help," answers Udugur. Turning to one of his riders, he shouts an order: "Bring him over here!" Then he turns back to Timucin.

"You see, the Tajin have been riding over our land for years, ignoring our borders. We would not go to war for that alone, but when we heard that they had attacked the Holy Mountain and spilled blood there, we had to act."

Not to mention that this gave you the excuse[4] you had been looking for, adds Timucin in his thoughts. Somehow, though, his mother seems to understand what he means and looks at him, terrified[5], as if he had said it aloud. The Lord of the Merkites, too, looks irritated.

It's the truth, though, says a scornful voice in the back of his head, *but your mother is right: You've got a lot to learn, little Khan.*

"Don't call me that!" growls Timucin, who suddenly realises that he has spoken these words out loud as the Merkite and his mother look at him.

"What should we call you?" asks Udugur.

1 **to count oneself lucky** – *sich zu den Glücklichen zählen*
2 **you would have been dead by now** – *du wärest schon tot*
3 **deaf** – *taub*
4 **excuse** – *Vorwand*
5 **terrified** – *erschrocken*

Ilhan arrives before he has to answer, and he is not alone. He has brought the men with him who were hiding amongst the rocks up the slope. Even one of the wounded men, so weak that his is leaning on another, has come. The men greet each other. There are many greetings and much patting on the shoulders[1]. Udugur even hugs Ilhan briefly with real joy, a sight that makes Timucin feel slightly ill[2]. Ilhan then walks towards Timucin and gives him the sword he left on the rocks. Although he does not throw it to Timucin's feet, the way in which he gives it to him makes it clear that he would rather have done that.

"You forgot this, my Khan," he says sneeringly[3].

Timucin takes the weapon from him without speaking, puts it back through his belt and turns to the Merkites.

"How did you know what had happened?"

Udugur turns and gestures impatiently. It takes a few moments before two of the Merkites come towards him with a third figure. Timucin almost shouts when he recognises who they are carrying. At first, he thinks that they may have taken him prisoner, but then he sees that they are probably supporting him more than anything. He can barely stand on his own.

"Chuzir!" Timucin jumps towards him and throws his arms so tightly around him that his feet almost lift off of the ground.

"That traitor!" shouts one of Üdschin's warriors. "Where did you find him?"

Udugur looks at his clansman confused, then shakes his head. He points to Chuzir, who is so pale that Timucin is suddenly afraid. He looks even sicker than he did a few days back.

"Traitor?" asks Udugur, surprised. He turns and speaks to Timucin.

"The boy had two arrows still in his back when he reached us. He was close to death, but he did not rest until we left to come and save you, Timucin."

1 **patting on the shoulders** – *Schulterklopfen*
2 **to make someone feel slightly ill** – *jdm. eine leichte Übelkeit verursachen*
3 **sneering** – *höhnisch*

"In his condition?" asks Üdschin. She turns to Chuzir: "That could have been the death of you, my boy."

"I said to you that I would repay my debt[1] to you," says Chuzir, struggling to speak.

"Even if you had died doing it, you fool?" asks Timucin.

Chuzir is too weak to reply again, but Udugur nods and adds: "Your friend has done even more, Timucin. Bring her to us."

"What did he do?" asks Timucin as his heart starts to beat louder again.

"There is a reason that we are so late," answers Udugur. "Your friend made us go to the barbarians in the North."

Timucin does not understand at all what is meant, and looks at Üdschin and then at Chuzir. He is about to ask the Merkite Lord what is going on, when the men once again make way and a single, slim female form appears. Despite the biting cold, her hood is down, allowing Timucin to see her thin face and the two thick black ponytails[2], plaited[3] and reaching down to her shoulders. He can see her beautiful eyes and his heart stops for a moment.

"Arbesa?" he whispers.

"You're friend insisted that we free her first," says Udugur. "And we'd have had to put him in chains[4] to stop him. He'd have probably broken through those too, though!"

Timucin can no longer listen to what he is being told. His heart is beating again, so fast and hard that he cannot breathe.

"Arbesa," he croaks[5], "is it… is it really you?"

There is something in her eyes that almost paralyses[6] him. It is the longing[7] that has ruled every moment of his life since she was taken away.

1 **repay a debt** – *eine Schuld zurückzahlen*
2 **ponytail** – *Zopf, Pferdeschwanz*
3 **plaited** – *geflochten*
4 **to put sb in chains** – *jdn. in Ketten legen*
5 **to croak** – *krächzen*
6 **to paralyse** – *lähmen*
7 **longing** – *Sehnsucht*

But there is something more, something he cannot understand. Is it fear? What of?

"You know what has happened to her in the last few years, don't you?" asks Udugur.

What does it matter? Arbesa is alive and back at his side, and that is all that counts. He wants to walk up to her and take her in his arms, but Udugur motions[1] to him to stay still.

"Is this the girl you were looking for?"

"Yes, that is her, Arbesa," says Timucin, "my bride."

As he says these last two words, it is as if a shadow appears over Udugur's face. His voice is different when he speaks again.

"She was promised to you, I know, but there a few things that you should know."

Timucin's heart starts to beat even faster than before. He looks at Arbesa and then at his mother and then at the Merkites. Then he looks back to Arbesa and understands what the Merkite means. This must be the reason for the fear so visible in Arbesa's eyes. She is not alone. She has something under her cloak, something small that is whimpering[2] quietly.

Timucin says nothing, but goes to her and opens her cloak, his fingers trembling. He stares down at the child, wrapped in warm blankets and pressed protectively against her chest. It cannot be more than a few months old.

"What… what is that?" he says, looking down at the bundle[3].

"It's a bastard[4], I assume," says Ilhan spitefully.

"Is it… is it true?" stammers Timucin. He looks at the child and waits for feelings to come, but nothing does. He feels empty. Arbesa looks at him, her eyes black and wide open with fear. She seems unable to speak,

1 **to motion to sb to do sth** – *jdm. anhand einer Geste etw. bedeuten*
2 **to whimper** – *wimmern*
3 **bundle** – *Bündel*
4 **bastard** – *außereheliches Kind*

and clutches[1] the child closer and closer to her chest. The child cries louder and louder.

"Is it true?" he asks again.

Arbesa nods. She still cannot speak, and suddenly Timucin understands where the ever-growing[2] fear in her eyes is coming from. The very thought stabs at his heart like the blade of a knife.

"You know what you have to do," says Ilhan.

No, Timucin does not, and he does not want to know either.

It is the way of the warrior, young Khan, whispers the dragon in his thoughts. *You must take it, and sooner or later you will.*

Why does Sarantuya think she knows what he will do?

Because that is the true power of the dragon, little Khan, answers Sarantuya, *the power to see what was, what is, and what will come to pass. You will become khan of your tribe, and later Genghis, the Khan of Khans, the ruler of the entire earth.*

But…

It has always been this way, and it always will be, says the dragon silently, sadly. *It's not your fault, my little Khan, for the gods who made you men did not just give you your wisdom, but also your weaknesses.*

"Timucin…" whispers Arbesa, finally breaking her silence. Her voice is little more than a whisper, so quiet that he is probably the only one to hear her speak. There is more in this one word than just his name. If his heart were not already broken, it would break now.

"Timucin," says his mother, too, while the dragon whispers in his thoughts: *Make your choice, my Khan.*

His hand creeps[3] under his cloak and clasps[4] the hilt of his sword. There it is, the power of the dragon, there to serve him and let him do whatever he sees fit. Nothing on earth can stop somebody who has this power – and he must pay the price for this power. Arbesa's eyes follow his movement, and perhaps it is what he sees in her eyes that is the most

1 **to clutch** – *an sich pressen, umklammern*
2 **ever-growing** – *immer größer werdend*
3 **to creep** – *kriechen*
4 **to clasp sth** – *sich um etw. schließen*

disturbing[1]. She knows what is coming – what he *has* to do! She is shaking with fear[2]. Her eyes are filled with sorrow[3] – but there is no hate. She bears him no ill will[4] at all. If she did hate him, he could stand it, but he cannot bear[5] this, the way she expects her fate and the fate of her newborn[6] child.

He removes his hand. Ilhan is not the only one who makes a noise of surprise.

"What are you doing, my boy?" asks Udugur.

"She is my bride[7]," says Timucin.

"She was your bride," shouts Ilhan, "but not now. Look at her! Nothing more than a plaything[8] for the Tajin and the Barbarians! And now she is carrying their bastard at her breast. Do you expect us to follow you while you raise this barbarian baby until it can rule[9] over us?"

Timucin looks him in the eyes and keeps his gaze fixed on him. But the young warrior not only returns his stare defiantly[10], but flashes his eyes back at him.

"He is right, Timucin," says Udugur. "Nobody will follow you if you choose her. You will not become khan."

"You know what you have to do," says Ilhan once more, "and if you do not want to do it yourself, then let me do it, my Khan. I would be happy to do your duty for you." His voice is dripping with scorn[11] as his hand falls to his belt and to the hilt of his sword.

"No," replies Timucin, "that will not be necessary."

1 **disturbing** – *verstörend*
2 **to shake with fear** – *vor Furcht zittern*
3 **sorrow** – *Trauer*
4 **to bear sb ill will** *(veraltet)* – *jdm. gram sein*
5 **to bear sth** – *etw. ertragen*
6 **newborn** – *neugeboren*
7 **bride** – *Braut*
8 **plaything** – *Spielzeug*
9 **to rule over sb** – *über jdn. herrschen*
10 **he returns his stare defiantly** – *er hält seinem Blick trotzig stand*
11 **dripping with scorn** – *triefend vor Hohn*

He draws his sword, and Arbesa draws the child closer to her. She closes her eyes resignedly.

There is utter silence. He lifts the weapon slowly, takes a small step towards Arbesa and then turns round, placing himself between her and Ilhan.

"Nobody shall touch her," he says, quietly and with a voice which, while shaky, gains in power and depth with every word he speaks. "Her child is also to be left alone. Does everybody understand? Arbesa is my bride, and she will be my wife before next spring. She will be the Lady of my clan."

"Which clan do you mean?" shouts Ilhan. "None of us will follow you if you choose her!"

"Ilhan!" says Üdschin, lacking the authority she usually has. Ilhan's eyes flash, but he does nothing more than purse his lips[1]. Then he speaks.

"I apologise, my Lady, but if your son takes up arms[2] against his own people to defend a bastard child, then he is not of our blood!" Sounds of agreement[3] can be heard. Ilhan continues confidently. "And if you choose to stand by him, then you are no longer our Lady."

Whispers spread through the crowd, and not all of them sound as if they are in agreement with Ilhan. Then again, nobody speaks out against him – and how can they? Timucin knows that this is the chance Ilhan has been waiting for. He knows what these men are thinking, and Üdschin too seems to understand. She is silent, but her face shows her horror[4]. She turns to Udugur, her eyes begging[5] him to do something. But he looks at her with nothing more than a brief shake of his head.

"The Tajin are our enemies to the death, the barbarians from the North, too," he says sadly.

Sarantuya, thinks Timucin, desperate. The dragon is silent, however, and the strength it gives him is gone too. Timucin feels very alone.

1 **to purse one's lips** – *die Lippen schürzen*
2 **to take up arms** – *die Waffe erheben*
3 **agreement** – *Zustimmung*
4 **horror** – *Entsetzen*
5 **to beg sb** – *jdn. anflehen*

"Nobody will touch her," he repeats, "neither her, nor the child!"

Ilhan's hand grasps the hilt of his sword more tightly, and Timucin can see his muscles tensing[1] beneath his cloak. He knows that he does not stand a chance against Ilhan – he may be smaller, but he is much more powerful. Nevertheless, Timucin straightens his back and shoulders.

"Stop it!" shouts Udugur. "Enough blood has been spilled, and I shall not sit back and see swords raised!"

Ilhan flashes his eyes at him, but takes his hand from his sword and turns to Timucin.

"I don't need a sword for this, anyway," he says.

Timucin is about to answer, but Arbesa speaks before him, touching his shoulder.

"He is right, Timucin, it is the child of a barbarian."

But it is also her child, a part of her, and as long as she has a place in his life, so will the child. He has already betrayed her once by deciding as a khan would and not as a boy should. He will never make this mistake again.

This is the way of the khan, my little friend, whispers the dragon, *the power of the dragon that you asked for is yours. You need only reach[2] for it and the world will be yours, Genghis.*

For a long time, Timucin stands staring at Ilhan – it feels like an eternity[3]. He looks at him and thinks he can see the eyes of the man he killed, the faces of his wife and children. Then he sees the green, lush land on the other side of Burchan Chaldun, just as the dragon promised it to him before she turned it dark and dry under her burning shadow. He does not want this scorched earth.

He puts his sword back through his belt, turns back to Arbesa and takes the child out of her arms, pressing it to him protectively. Timucin is not good with children, and the newborn starts to cry in way that makes

1 **to tense** – *sich spannen*
2 **to reach for sth** – *nach etw. greifen*
3 **eternity** – *Ewigkeit*

him feel helpless. He feels a new tenderness[1] for the small being in his arms. He stretches out a hand to Arbesa.

"Shall we go?" he asks.

She looks at him, confused. And although she takes his hand, it is as if it is only a reflex – out of obedience.

"None of us will try and stop you," says Udugur, both as a promise to Timucin and an order to his own men, "but you should think about this carefully. No clan will take you in. There is no place for this child in the yurts of the Merkites."

"Then we will start our own clan," answers Timucin, just like he said to Chuzir a week back. Now, however, it is no joke.

"The Clan of the Pigs, I suppose," laughs Ilhan, only to be surprised by Üdschin as she slaps him across the face[2]. He stumbles back a few steps and his eyes flash with hate. Timucin is sure that it is only the fact that Udugur and the Merkites are there that stops him from leaping at her.

"Yours will be a very small clan," says Udugur, "a clan of three."

"Four," adds Chuzir, weakly but clearly. Üdschin shakes her head, smiles, and corrects him: "Five!"

Udugur says nothing more, but seems sad. He stands aside to let the new khan and clan through. He is right, thinks Timucin. His is a very small clan. Really it is not a clan at all, but rather a mix of lost, homeless, friendless people without a future.

DRACHENFRAGE

What does everyone expect Timucin to do with the baby – and why?

You could have had the world, whispers Sarantuya.

The world? *The world?* He has a family: his mother, his wife, his friend, a child – who needs the world? Let another become Genghis.

They leave, and deep inside, he can feel the smile of the dragon.

1 **tenderness** – *Zärtlichkeit*
2 **to slap sb across the face** – *jdm. eine Ohrfeige verpassen*

Fantasy-Vokabular

assault *Angriff*

armour *Rüstung, Harnisch*

attack *Angriff*

arrow, bow and quiver *Pfeil, Bogen und Köcher*

to release sb from an oath *jmd. von einem Eid entbinden*

darkness *Finsternis*

to banish sb *jdn. verbannen, verjagen*

bandit *Räuber*

coward *Feigling*

creature *Wesen*

battle *Schlacht*

combat *Kampf*

brave *wacker, mutig*

castle *Schloss*

dragon *Drache*

to beg forgiveness *um Vergebung bitten*

noble *edel*

to mount a horse *auf ein Pferd aufsteigen*

to hallucinate *fantasieren*

to put sb in chains *jmd. in Ketten legen*

realm *Reich*

resistance *Widerstand*

magical *verzaubert*

wasteland *Ödnis*

to quake *beben, zittern*

legend *Mythos*

pitiless *gnadenlos*

defender *Verteidiger*

spark *Funke*

to rule *herrschen*

tribe *Sippe, Stamm*

fellow *Gefährte*

ruin *Untergang*

to lay waste to sth *etw. verwüsten*

leader *Anführer*

to fight valiantly *sich tapfer schlagen*

to pillage *plündern*

to spill blood *Blut vergießen*

to swear allegiance to sb *jdm. Gefolgschaft schwören*

traitor *Verräter*

to harry *verheeren, plündern*

wisdom *Weisheit*

to curse oneself *sich verfluchen*

Englisch-deutsche Wortliste

a great many	*sehr viele*
a little further	*ein bisschen weiter*
abyss	*Abgrund, Kluft, Schlucht*
accident	*Unfall*
accompany	*begleiten*
accusing	*anklagend*
act	*handeln*
additional	*weitere*
admit	*eingestehen*
advance-guard	*Vorhut*
advice	*Rat*
against one's will	*gegen jdns. Willen*
agility	*Geschmeidigkeit*
agree with sb	*jdm. zustimmen*
agreement	*Zustimmung*
all his fault	*allein seine Schuld*
all the more difficult	*umso schwerer*
almost without realising that he is doing so	*beinahe ohne eigenes Zutun*
although he knew what he would see	*obwohl er wusste, was er sehen würde*
amusement	*Vergnügen*
and so has the view from up there	*ebenso wie der Blick von dort oben*
anger	*Wut, Zorn*
anger is welling up	*Wut kocht hoch*
anxious	*beklommen, ängstlich*
any other given	*jedes beliebige*
apply pressure	*Druck ausüben*
Are you dissatisfied with...?	*Missfällt dir ...?*
armour	*Panzer, Harnisch, Rüstung*
armpit	*Achsel*
army	*Armee*
arrow	*Pfeil*
as ever	*wie eh und je*
as if by chance	*als wäre es Zufall*
as if he has been struck by lightning	*wie vom Blitz getroffen*
as if it were bathed in the midday sun	*als wäre es in das Licht der Mittagssonne getaucht*
as it was once customary to do	*wie es früher Sitte war*
as though	*als ob*
as you should	*wie es sich gehört*
assign sb to sth	*jdn. zu etw. abstellen, jdm. etw. übertragen*
at length	*lange*
at the very end	*ganz am Ende, am äußersten Ende*
attacker	*Angreifer*
attempt	*Versuch*
await sb (veraltet)	*auf jdn. warten*
awe-inspiring	*furchteinflößend*
awful	*schrecklich*
back then	*damals*
banish a thought (Redewendung)	*einen Gedanken verscheuchen*
Barbarian tribe	*Barbarenstamm*
bare ground	*nackter Boden*
barren	*öde*
bathed in light	*lichtdurchflutet*
battle	*Schlacht*
be alert	*auf der Hut sein*
be appropriate to a khan	*eines Khans würdig sein*

be bothered by	*sich Gedanken machen um*
be directly responsible for sth	*die unmittelbare Schuld an etw. tragen*
be good fortune	*pures Glück sein*
be gripped by fear	*von Angst gepackt werden*
be headed somewhere	*irgendwo hin unterwegs sein*
be heard	*zu hören*
be in a hurry	*es eilig haben*
be in the mood for sth	*der Sinn nach etw. stehen*
be lucky	*Glück haben*
be of use	*etw. bewirken, etw. nützen*
be shaped by	*geprägt sein von*
be told off	*gescholten werden*
be true of sb/sth	*für jmd./etw. gelten, zutreffen*
be upset	*bestürzt, aufgeregt, traurig sein*
be worthy of a khan	*eines Khans würdig sein*
bear sb ill-will (veraltet)	*jdm. gram sein*
bear sth	*etw. ertragen*
beard	*Bart*
beat sb to death	*jdn. erschlagen*
beat up	*verprügeln*
beat wildly	*wild klopfen*
beckon sb to oneself	*jdn. zu sich winken*
bedding	*Bettzeug, Schlafplatz*
beg forgiveness	*um Vergebung bitten*
beg sb	*jdn. anflehen*
belongings	*Besitz, Hab und Gut*
bend forward	*sich vorbeugen*
bent over	*gebückt*
beside the point	*nebensächlich*
betray	*verraten*
betrayal	*Verrat*
beyond	*jenseits*
beyond all measure	*maßlos*
bitch	*Hündin*
blade	*Klinge*
blank look	*verständnisloser Blick*
blanket	*Decke*
bleed	*bluten*
blink	*blinzeln*
bloodshed	*Sterben, Blutvergießen*
blurred	*verschwommen*
bolt	*davonlaufen*
bolt upright	*hoch aufgerichtet*
bonds	*Fesseln*
bony fingers	*dürre, knochige Finger*
booming voice	*dröhnende Stimme*
bottom	*(hier) Talsohle*
bottom lip	*Unterlippe*
bound	*Satz*
boundless	*grenzenlos*
bow	*Bogen*
bow to sb	*sich vor jdm. beugen*
bowstring	*Sehne eines Bogens*
branch	*Ast*
brash	*ungestüm*
brave, bravery	*tapfer, Tapferkeit*
bride	*Braut*
brief	*flüchtig*
brink	*Kante*
brother in oath	*Schwurbruder*
bundle	*Bündel*
burning curiosity	*brennende Neugier*
busily	*emsig, geschäftig*
but then	*aber schließlich*

butcher	*niedermetzeln*
by the way	*nebenbei, beiläufig*
calm	*ruhig, entspannt*
campsite	*Lager*
careful	*behutsam, sorgfältig*
careless	*leichtsinnig, unachtsam*
carelessness	*Unvorsichtigkeit, Nachlässigkeit*
carnage	*Gemetzel*
catch	*fangen, aufgreifen*
cause	*Grund, Anlass*
cause sb pain	*jdm. Schmerzen zufügen*
challengers	*Herausforderer*
chatter (teeth)	*klappern (mit den Zähnen)*
cheek	*Wange*
chew	*kauen*
childish	*kindisch*
chunky	*untersetzt*
clang	*klirren, klingen*
clash	*Zusammenstoß*
clasp	*umklammern*
claw	*Kralle*
cliff face	*Klippenwand*
cling to sth	*sich an etw. festklammern*
cloak	*Mantel, Umhang*
clutch	*an sich pressen, umklammern*
come loose	*sich lösen*
comfort sb	*jdn. beruhigen, trösten*
congratulate sb	*jdn. beglückwünschen*
conscious	*bewusst*
considerably	*erheblich*
considerate	*rücksichtsvoll*
conspicuous	*auffällig*
constantly	*ununterbrochen*
control oneself	*sich (mühsam) beherrschen*
convincing	*überzeugend*
cord	*Strick*
count oneself lucky	*sich zu den Glücklichen zählen*
counter	*widersprechen, erwidern*
countless	*zahllos*
courage	*Mut*
cower in fear	*sich vor Furcht krümmen*
crackle	*prasseln*
creature	*Geschöpf*
creep	*kriechen*
croak	*krächzen*
croaking	*krächzend*
crone	*alte Hexe, Schrulle*
crouch	*in die Hocke gehen*
cruel	*grausam*
crush	*zerschmettern*
cry of battle	*Schlachtruf*
curious	*neugierig*
curl to a fist	*sich zu einer Faust ballen*
curse oneself	*sich verfluchen*
curt	*spröde, schroff*
custom	*Sitte*
dare	*wagen*
darken	*verfinstern, sich trüben*
dawn	*Morgendämmerung*
deaf	*taub*
debt	*Schuld*
decide not to hear	*vorziehen, etw. nicht zu hören*

decide the fate of sth	*über das Schicksal von etw. entscheiden*
decided	*entschlossen*
deduction	*Schlussfolgerung*
deeds	*Taten*
defeat	*besiegen*
defiance	*Trotz , Auflehnung*
defiant	*trotzig*
delicious	*köstlich*
demonstratively	*demonstrativ*
depth	*Tiefe*
desert sth	*etw. verlassen*
despair	*Verzweiflung*
die, dying	**sterben**
disappear	*verschwinden*
disappointed	*enttäuscht*
disarmed	*entwaffnet*
disaster	*Unglück*
disbelieving	*ungläubig*
dishonour	*entehren*
dismissive	*abfällig*
disquiet	*Unbehagen*
disrespectful	*respektlos, verächtlich*
distorted	*verzerrt*
disturbing	*verstörend*
dizzy	*schwindelig, benommen*
do as sb says	*auf jdn. hören*
do business	*Geschäfte machen*
do damage	*Schaden anrichten*
doe	*Reh*
don't worry	*keine Sorge*
doubt sth	*etw. bezweifeln*
dozen	*Dutzend*
draw (a sword)	*(Schwert) ziehen*
dried black	*schwarz geronnen*
dripping with scorn	*triefend vor Hohn*
drop one's gaze	*den Blick senken*
drown sb out	*jdns. Stimme übertönen*
due to	*wegen*
duty	*Pflicht*
Each piece of wood they brought back has been paid for in blood.	*Jedes Stück Holz, das sie mitgebracht haben, wurde mit Blut bezahlt.*
edible	*essbar*
effort	*Anstrengung*
elbow sb	*jdm. mit dem Ellbogen ins Gesicht stoßen*
embarrass sb	*jdn. in Verlegenheit bringen*
embers	*Glut*
embrace	*Umarmung*
emerge	*heraustreten*
emotional	*aufwühlend*
encouraging	*aufmunternd*
enthusiastic	*begeistert*
entrust sth to sb	*jdm. etw. anvertrauen*
erase	*löschen, verwischen*
escape sb's notice	*jdm. verborgen bleiben*
eternity	*Ewigkeit*
evasively	*ausweichend*
even those that you do not know about	*selbst die, die nicht einmal du kennst*
ever growing	*immer größer werdend*
evergreen pastures	*unerschöpfliche Weidegründe*
every now and then	*ab und zu*
everything except	*alles außer*
examine	*unter die Lupe nehmen, prüfen, untersuchen*

excel at sth	*sich in etw. hervortun*
excuse	*Vorwand*
exhaust oneself	*sich erschöpfen*
exhausted	*erschöpft*
expecting to	*darauf gefasst*
expression	*Miene, Gesichtsausdruck*
extremely	*äußerst*
fabric	*Stoff*
faithful	*treu*
fake sth	*etw. simulieren*
famine	*Hungersnot*
far out of one's reach	*unerreichbar fern*
fate	*Schicksal*
feature	*Gesichtszug; auch: Merkmal*
feel forced to do sth	*sich zu etw. genötigt fühlen*
fell	*fällen*
fellow	*Gefährte*
fertile soil	*fruchtbarer Boden*
fever	*Fieber*
fight against sth	*gegen etw. kämpfen*
firewood	*Brennholz*
fit	*angemessen sein, passend sein*
flash	*blitzen*
flash one's eyes at sb	*jdn. anfunkeln*
flat slope	*flacher Hugel*
flee	*fliehen*
flicker	*flackern*
flinch	*zusammenzucken, zurückzucken*
flourish	*gedeihen*
flurry	*Gestöber*
footsteps	*Schritte*
for as long as he can remember (Redewendung)	*solange er denken kann*

for nothing	*ohne Grund, von ungefähr*
for sure	*ganz sicher, bestimmt*
for want of anything else	*in ihrer Not*
forbidden	*verboten*
force sth on sb	*jdm. etw. aufzwingen*
forgive sb	*jdm. verzeihen*
form	*Form; hier: Gestalt*
for sure	*ganz sicher, bestimmt*
fortress	*Festung*
found	*gründen*
fragile	*gebrechlich*
freeze to death	*erfrieren*
frighten	*erschrecken, ängstigen*
from head to toe (Redewendung)	*von Kopf bis Fuß*
from time to time	*dann und wann, ab und zu*
frown	*die Stirn runzeln*
frozen stiff	*steif gefroren*
fur	*Pelz*
fury	*Zorn*
gasp	*japsen*
gather	*sich zusammentun, zusammenlaufen*
gaunt	*eingefallen*
generous	*großzügig*
Genghis	*Gemeint ist Dschingis Khan. Auf Englisch kann er wie im Deutschen mit dsch am Anfang oder mit g gesprochen werden.*
gentle	*sachte, sanft*
gesture to sb	*jdm. etw. bedeuten*
get away	*entkommen*

get back to sleep	*wieder einschlafen*
get worried about nothing (Redewendung)	*sich umsonst Sorgen machen*
ghost like figures	*Schemen*
ghostly	*geistergleich, schemenhaft*
gigantic	*riesig*
give sb a thorough once over	*jdn. prüfend, durchdringend ansehen*
give sth up	*auf etw. verzichten*
glisten	*glänzen*
glory	*Ruhm, Glanz*
grab for sth	*nach etw. greifen*
grab on	*greifen nach, festhalten an*
graceful	*anmutig*
grant sb sth	*jdm. etw. gewähren*
grateful	*dankbar*
grave	*ernst*
graze	*Schramme*
grind	*knirschen*
grip	*festhalten*
grit one's teeth	*die Zähne zusammenbeißen*
growl	*brummen, knurren*
grumpy	*mürrisch*
guard	*hüten*
guess	*erahnen, raten*
gulp sth down	*etw. gierig herunterschlucken*
gust of wind	*Windstoß, Windböe*
habit	*Angewohnheit*
hair's breadth	*Haaresbreite*
hallucinate	*halluzinieren, fantasieren*
hand's width	*Handbreite*
harm sb	*jdm. schaden*
harmonious	*ebenmäßig*
harrow (veraltet)	*verheeren, zerstören*
harsh	*hart, forsch*
haste	*Hast, Eile*
hasty	*überhastet, hastig*
hateful	*hasserfüllt*
haunt sb	*jdn. heimsuchen*
have an obligation	*eine Verpflichtung haben*
have difficulty doing sth	*schwerfallen, etw. zu tun*
have energy left over	*überschüssige Kräfte haben*
have the shivers	*frösteln*
have the upper hand	*die Oberhand haben*
hazy outline	*verschwommener Umriss*
He can see his mind working.	*Er kann sehen, wie es hinter seiner Stirn arbeitet.*
He could say quite a lot in reply.	*Er könnte vieles antworten.*
He doesn't grow claws or wings.	*Ihm wachsen keine Klauen oder Schwingen.*
he had seemed to be avoiding	*er schien auszuweichen*
he had to almost force him to	*er musste ihn fast dazu zwingen*
He has never forgiven himself for his treachery.	*Er hat sich diesen Verrat nie verziehen.*
he is close to telling	*er ist kurz davor, es zu sagen*
he is overcome with sth	*ihn überkommt etw.*
he of all people	*ausgerechnet er*
he really should be heading back	*er sollte wirklich zurückgehen*

He regrets these words even while he is saying them. *Er bedauert diese Worte schon, bevor er sie ausgesprochen hat.*

He returns his stare defiantly. *Er hält seinem Blick trotzig stand.*

He would not have contradicted her. *Er hätte ihr nicht widersprochen.*

He would rather have said more. *Er hätte lieber mehr gesagt.*

head towards sth *auf dem Weg sein zu*

healer *Heilkundiger*

heap *Haufen*

heir *Erbe*

hilt of the dagger *Dolchgriff*

hiss *zischen*

hoarse *heiser*

honour *Ehre*

hood *Kapuze*

hoof *Huf*

hopeless *hoffnungslos*

horde *Horde*

horror *Entsetzen*

hug *drücken, herzen*

humiliate *demütigen*

hurry (up) *sich beeilen*

hurt sb *jdn. verletzen, jdm. wehtun*

if it goes on like this *wenn es so weiter geht*

I have not chosen it. *Ich habe es nicht gewählt.*

I should have known *ich hätte wissen sollen*

I should never have done it. *Ich hätte das nicht tun dürfen.*

I suppose it was my fault. *Es war wohl meine Schuld.*

I would have liked nothing more than for her to be... *Nichts hätte mein Herz mehr erfreut als dass sie ... gewesen/geworden wäre*

imaginary friend *unsichtbarer Freund*

impenetrable *undurchdringlich*

impetuous *ungestüm*

imposing *imposant, beeindruckend*

impress *beeindrucken*

impressive *beeindruckend*

improvised *improvisiert*

in a mood for jokes *zu Scherzen aufgelegt*

in his mind's eye (Redewendung) *vor seinem inneren Auge*

inaudible *unhörbar*

including *einschließlich, mitgerechnet*

influence *beeinflussen*

injury *Verletzung*

insist *beharren*

insist that sb does sth *darauf bestehen, dass jmd. etw. macht*

intend to do sth *sich etw. fest vornehmen*

interpret *auslegen, deuten*

interrupt *unterbrechen*

iron *Eisen, eisern*

Is that your idea of fun? (Redewendung) *Ist das eure Art von Humor?*

It is for the better. (Redewendung) *Es ist auch besser so.*

It is the least of his worries. (Redewendung) *Das war seine geringste Sorge.*

it pains me to say it (Redewendung, veraltet)	*ich sage es nur ungern*
it seems ten times longer	*es kommt ihm zehnmal so lange vor*
It sends a chill down his spine. (Redewendung)	*Ihm läuft ein kalter Schauer über den Rücken.*
it's none of my business	*das ist nicht meine Angelegenheit, das geht mich nichts an*
jagged	*schartig, gezackt, scharfkantig*
judging by sth	*nach etw. zu schließen*
keep close to sb	*an jdm. dranbleiben*
keep doing sth	*etw. weiterhin tun*
keep falling	*weiterhin fallen*
keep one's cool	*die Ruhe bewahren*
keep sth away from oneself	*sich etw. vom Leib zu halten*
khan	*Khan (Häuptling eines Steppenvolkes; im Englischen wird khan nur in der Anrede groß geschrieben, z. B. „Forgive me, my Khan!")*
kidnap	*entführen*
kidnapping	*Entführung*
kneel down	*sich niederknien*
lack sth	*an etw. mangeln*
lad	*Junge, Bursche*
Lady Khan	*weibl. Khan*
lap	*Schoß*
lay waste to	*verheeren, verwüsten, zerstören*
laying waste to whatever comes in their path	*sie zerstören alles, was in ihren Weg gerät*
leader	*Anführer*
leap at sb	*sich auf jdn. stürzen*
leather armour	*Harnisch*
leave sb high and dry	*jdn. im Stich lassen*
let alone	*geschweige denn*
lifeless	*leblos*
like a whip	*wie eine Peitsche*
liven sb up	*jdns Lebensgeister wecken*
livestock	*Vieh*
long past	*lange vorbei*
longing	*Sehnsucht*
look at sb blankly	*jdn. verständnislos anblicken*
look daggers at sb	*jdn. mit Blicken durchbohren*
look nothing like	*etw./jdm. nicht ähnlich sehen, nicht aussehen wie*
look sheepish	*ein schuldbewusstes/verlegenes Gesicht machen*
lose one's balance	*das Gleichgewicht verlieren*
lose one's grip	*seinen Halt verlieren*
lower sth	*etw. senken, etw. sinken lassen*
loyal	*treu*
lush	*saftig, sattgrün*
magical	*magisch, verzaubert*
make a fool out of oneself	*sich lächerlich machen*
make good hunting and riding	*zum Jagen und Reiten einladen*
make progress	*vorankommen*
make someone feel slightly ill	*jdm. eine leichte Übelkeit verursachen*
make up for sth	*etw. wiedergutmachen*

make way for sb	*jdm. den Weg freigeben*
manage to do sth	*etw. zustande bringen, es schaffen, etw. zu machen*
manage to say	*etw. herausbekommen (Wörter)*
masked	*vermummt*
meadow	*Wiese*
meek	*kleinlaut*
mind	*Gedanken, Geist*
mischievous	*verschmitzt*
misery	*Elend, Not*
misplaced	*fehl am Platz*
mist	*Nebel, Dunst*
misuse	*missbrauchen*
morass	*Morast*
motion to sb to do sth	*jdm. anhand einer Geste etw. bedeuten*
mount (a horse)	*aufsitzen (auf ein Pferd)*
move out	*aufbrechen*
murder	*ermorden*
murmur	*murmeln*
muster (force)	*(seine Kräfte) zusammennehmen*
narrow	*schmal*
nasty	*gemein*
necessarily	*zwangsläufig*
necessary	*nötig*
newborn	*neugeboren*
nightmare	*Albtraum*
no longer bothering to hide her contempt	*nun in eindeutig verächtlichem Ton*
no sign of sth	*von etw. keine Spur*
noble	*nobel, ritterlich*
none of the faces	*keines der Gesichter*
nonsense	*Unsinn*
not bother to do sth	*sich es sparen, etw. zu tun; sich nicht die Mühe geben, etw. zu tun*
not least	*nicht zuletzt*
nothingness	*Nichts*
numb	*taub, betäubt*
oan	*ächzen*
obedient	*gehorsam*
obey	*gehorchen*
object	*protestieren, Einwände erheben*
obscure	*bedecken*
obvious	*selbstverständlich*
odd	*sonderbar, seltsam*
of use	*von Nutzen*
on my behalf	*meinetwegen, in meinem Auftrag*
onwards	*weiter (voran)*
opportunity	*Gelegenheit*
order	*Befehl*
otherwise	*sonst*
outnumber	*in der Überzahl sein*
outnumbered	*unterlegen (Zahl)*
outstretched	*ausgestreckt*
owe sb sth	*jdm. etw. schulden*
pale	*bleich, blass, hell*
pant	*keuchen*
paralyse	*lähmen*
parchment	*Pergament*
part of life	*Teil des Lebens*
pass	*Hohlweg, Bergpass*
pass	*bestehen*
passionately	*leidenschaftlich, inbrünstig*
path	*Pfad, Weg*
patting on the shoulders	*Schulterklopfen*

pay dearly	*etw. teuer bezahlen*
peak	*Gipfel*
people	*ein Volk; Leute*
petulant	*patzig*
pick up	*aufnehmen*
piercing gaze	*durchdringender Blick*
pit	*Grube*
pitiless	*gnadenlos*
plain	*Ebene*
plaited	*geflochten*
plaything	*Spielzeug*
ponytail	*Zopf, Pferdeschwanz*
pound	*zertrampeln, schlagen, trommeln*
pretend	*so tun, als ob*
pride	*Stolz*
prisoner	*Gefangener*
prolong sth	*verlängern*
promise	*versprechen*
proof	*Beweis*
protect sb	*jdn. schützen*
protected	*geschützt*
protective	*behütsam*
proud	*stolz*
purse one's lips	*die Lippen schürzen*
pursue	*verfolgen, jagen*
put out	*löschen*
put sb in chains	*jdn. in Ketten legen*
quiver	*Köcher (für Pfeile)*
rage	*Zorn*
ransom	*Lösegeld*
razor-sharp	*messerscharf, scharf wie eine Rasierklinge*
reach	*erreichen*
reach for sth	*nach etw. greifen*
realm (veraltet)	*Reich*
reason	*Vernunft*
recapture sb	*jdn. wieder gefangen nehmen*
recover	*sich erholen*
regal gesture	*herrische Geste*
regret sth	*etw. bedauern*
rein	*Zügel*
reinforcements (military)	*Verstärkung*
release (from oath, bonds)	*entbinden (von einem Eid, von Fesseln)*
relieved	*beruhigt, erleichtert*
repay a debt	*eine Schuld zurückzahlen*
repel	*zurückschlagen (einen Angriff, Angreifer)*
reproach	*Tadel*
reproof	*Verweis*
resigned	*ergeben, schicksalsergeben, resigniert*
resist temptation	*einer Versuchung widerstehen*
resist the urge to	*dem Wunsch widerstehen*
resistance	*Widerstand*
rest	*Ruhe, Erholung*
rested	*ausgeruht*
retire	*hier: sich zurückziehen; auch: in den Ruhestand gehen*
rhetorical	*rhetorisch*
ride sb down	*jdn. niedertrampeln*
ridiculous	*lächerlich*
risk one's neck (Redewendung)	*Kopf und Kragen riskieren*
rock-covered	*mit Steinen bedeckt*
roll	*hier: sich wälzen; auch: rollen*

rotten leftovers	*verfaulte Abfälle*
rub	*reiben*
ruin	*Untergang, Ruin*
rule over sb	*über jdn. herrschen*
rumble (stomach)	*knurren (Magen)*
run one's fingers over sth	*etw. abtasten*
run out	*ausgehen, leer sein*
rush off	*davoneilen*
rustle	*Rauschen*
sacred	*heilig*
sacrifice	*opfern*
saddle	*Sattel*
sadder (sad, sadder, saddest)	*trauriger (traurig, trauriger, am traurigsten)*
sarcastic	*sarkastisch, abfällig*
sardonic	*höhnisch, hämisch*
satisfaction	*Zufriedenheit*
save sth	*sparen*
scaled	*geschuppt*
scant	*spärlich*
scattered to the four winds	*in alle Winde zerstreut*
sceptical	*misstrauisch, skeptisch*
scorch	*verbrennen, versengen*
scrape	*scharren*
scream piercingly	*gellend schreien*
screech	*kreischen*
scrub	*Buschwerk*
search for cover	*Schutz suchen*
search party	*Suchtrupp*
sense of direction	*Orientierungssinn*
senses	*Sinne*
set in	*anfangen, einsetzen*
set off	*aufbrechen, losgehen*
shady grove	*schattiger Hain*
shake one's head	*den Kopf schütteln*
shake one's pursuers off	*seine Verfolger abschütteln*
shake with fear	*vor Furcht zittern*
shaky	*bebend, zitterig*
shameless	*unverschämt*
sharp	*scharf*
She can hardly stop herself. (Redewendung)	*Sie kann sich nur noch mit Mühe davon abhalten.*
She is clutching at straws. (Redewendung)	*Das ist nur ein frommer Wunsch.*
sheath	*einstecken*
sheath a sword	*ein Schwert in die Scheide stecken*
sheer disbelief	*schierer/reiner Unglauben*
shield	*der Schild*
shoulder blades	*Schulterblätter*
shrug one's shoulders	*die Achseln zucken, die Schultern heben*
sigh	*seufzen*
sign of weakness	*ein Zeichen von Schwäche*
silence	*zum Schweigen bringen*
silent whisper	*lautloses Flüstern*
silly game	*Spielchen, dummes Spiel*
sit cross legged	*im Schneidersitz sitzen*
size sb up	*jdm. mit den Augen messen, jdn. mustern*
slap sb across the face	*jdm. eine Ohrfeige verpassen*
slide	*rutschen*
slight, tired nod	*leichtes, müdes Nicken*

slim	*schlank*
slip	*verrutschen*
slip unseen	*schleichen*
slow one's pace	*langsamer werden*
slowly but surely	*ebenso langsam wie unaufhaltsam*
slumber	*Schlummer*
smiling	*lächelnd*
smirk	*feixen; Grinsen*
smoulder	*lodern*
snap	*fauchen, schnappen*
sneering	*höhnisch*
snow flurries	*Schneegestöber*
soak	*tränken*
soar	*emporragen*
sob	*Schluchzen*
soft	*sanft*
sorrow	*Trauer*
spark	*Funke*
spat	*Kampf*
spite	*Schadenfreude, Gehässigkeit*
spiteful	*schadenfroh, gehässig*
splutter	*stottern*
spoil	*verhunzen*
spread	*ausbreiten*
stab	*stechen, mit der Klinge stoßen*
stammer	*stottern, stammeln*
stamp out the fire	*das Feuer austreten*
stand sth	*etw. aushalten, ertragen*
stare at sb	*jdn. anstarren*
start	*hier: zusammenzucken, auffahren; auch: beginnen*
steal, stole stolen	*stehlen*
stick in one's throat	*jdn. wurmen*
sticky	*klebrig*
storm	*stürmen*
storm off	*davonstürmen*
straighten up	*sich aufrichten*
stream	*Bach*
struggle	*kämpfen, sich abmühen, ringen*
struggle with oneself	*mit sich ringen*
stubborn	*störrisch, hartnäckig*
stumble	*stolpern*
stupidity	*Dummheit*
subside	*erlöschen, nachlassen*
suffer	*leiden*
summery	*sommerlich*
summon up	*all seinen Mut zusammennehmen*
superhuman	*übermenschlich*
supplies	*Vorräte*
suppress a smile	*sich ein Lächeln verkneifen*
surly	*mürrisch*
survive	*überleben*
survivor	*Überlebender*
suspicious	*misstrauisch*
swear allegiance to sb	*jdm. Treue, Gefolgschaft schwören*
swirls of snow and mist	*Wirbel aus Schnee und Nebel*
take	*nehmen; auch: erobern, stürmen*
take back one's words	*seine Worte zurücknehmen*
take offense at sth	*sich von etw. beleidigen lassen*
take the initiative	*die Initiative übernehmen*
take up arms	*die Waffe erheben*

take up posts	*sich postieren*
talk to oneself	*Selbstgespräche führen*
tear him into shreds	*ihn in Stücke reißen*
teasing	*neckisch*
tell sb who is boss	*jdn. in seine Schranken weisen.*
tempting	*verführerisch*
tenderness	*Zärtlichkeit*
tense	*angespannt*
terrible misfortune	*großes Unglück*
terrified	*erschrocken*
than can be expected	*als zu erwarten wäre*
that he had better do it sooner than later	*dass er es besser früher als später machen muss*
That's a new one.	*Das ist neu.*
the light is fading	*es dämmert*
then again	*andererseits, schließlich*
there is nothing of the sort	*so etwas gibt es nicht*
There is steam coming out of it.	*Es dampft.*
the way that I can take you	*den Weg, den ich dir eröffnen kann*
They can flee no further. (veraltet)	*Ihre Flucht endet hier.*
They cannot help but... (Redewendung)	*Sie können nicht umhin zu ...*
They don't say it for nothing. (Redewendung)	*Sie sagen das nicht von ungefähr.*
they haven't made much of an effort (Redewendung)	*sie haben sich keine besondere Mühe gegeben*
They step up.	*Sie treten zu ihm.*
thick, low cloud cover	*schwere, tief hängende Wolken*
Things may have happened differently.	*Vieles wäre vielleicht anders gekommen.*
think sb mad	*jdn. für verrückt halten*
think twice about doing sth (Redewendung)	*es sich zweimal überlegen, ob man etw. macht*
This does not change the fact that...	*Das ändert nichts an der Tatsache, dass ...*
this very spot	*genau hier*
thunder	*donnern*
thundering	*donnernd*
tie sb down	*jdn. fesseln*
tied up	*zusammengebunden*
tight	*fest*
to his relief	*zu seiner Erleichterung*
too much of a coward to admit	*zu feige, zuzugeben*
torture	*quälen*
toss and turn	*sich hin und her werfen*
tracks	*Spur*
trail off	*verstummen*
trails	*Spuren*
traitor	*Verräter*
trap	*Hinterhalt, Falle*
trapped	*eingefangen*
treachery	*Verrat*
treat sb well	*jdn. gut behandeln*
tremble	*zittern*
trembling	*zitterig*
tribe	*Sippe*
trust sb	*jdm. trauen*
try to get at sth	*auf etw. hinauswollen*
turn on one's heal	*auf dem Absatz herumfahren*

turn out to be true *sich als richtig erweisen*
uncanny *unheimlich*
uncomfortable silence *bedrücktes Schweigen*
unconquerable *uneinnehmbar*
undisguised *unverhohlen*
unharmed *unversehrt*
unidentifiable *unidentifizierbar*
unleash the full fury of the dragon *die volle Macht des Drachen entfesseln*
unwilling *widerstrebend*
upset *betroffen*
vicious *bösartig*
violently *heftig, gewaltig*
visible *sichtbar*
warrior *Krieger*
wasteland *Ödnis*
watchmen *Wachmänner*
wave away *wegschicken*
wavy *hügelig*
we are even *wir sind quitt*
We would all perish. (veraltet) *Es wäre unser aller Tod.*
wealthy *vermögend*
weapon *Waffe*
well meaning *gut gemeint, gutmütig*
well up *aufwallen*
What do you mean by that? *Was soll das denn heißen?*
What is the meaning of this? (Redewendung, veraltet) *Was hat das zu bedeuten?*
whimper *wimmern*
whip *peitschen; Peitsche*
whom *den, die*
whom he has assumed to be dead *die er für tot gehalten hat*
willing *bereit, willens*
wince *zusammenzucken*
wisdom *Weisheit*
with agility quite remarkable for her age *mit ziemlich bemerkenswerter Geschmeidigkeit für ihr Alter*
with a wink *augenzwinkernd*
with deep conviction *tief überzeugt*
with his knees drawn to his chest *mit angezogenen Knien/Beinen*
without a moment's thought (Redewendung) *ohne mit der Wimper zu zucken*
without hesitating *ohne zu zögern*
worried *besorgt*
wounded *verletzt*
wrap sth around oneself *sich in etw. einwickeln*
wrapped up *eingehüllt*
yell *schreien, brüllen*
yoke *Joch*
Your friend is being taken care of. *Für deinen Freund ist gesorgt.*
you would have been dead by now *du wärest schon tot*
yurt (tent) *Jurte (Zelt)*

Aufgaben

The Prophecy

1 – Tribe life

Folgende Vokabeln sind wichtig, um die Lebensweise der Steppeklans zu beschreiben. Kannst du sie mit den richtigen deutschen Übersetzungen verbinden?

1. tribe
2. livestock
3. belongings
4. warrior
5. fur

a) Krieger
b) Hab und Gut
c) Pelz
d) Sippe
e) Vieh

2 – The Holy Mountain

Timucin sucht Rat auf dem Heiligen Berg, der den Steppesippen als Ort der Götter gilt. Welches Wort benutzt er, um so einen Ort zu beschreiben? Es fängt mit *s* an.

____

3 – On the brink

Tollkühn steht Timucin am Abgrund, nicht mal einen Schritt vom Fall in die Nebel entfernt. Füll folgende Sätze mit den passenden Wörtern ein: Als Erinnerungshilfe steht der erste Buchstabe.

1. Timucin stands on the e ____________ of the moutain plateau.
2. He is on the brink of the a ____________.
3. He almost loses his g ____________ and climbs back from the b ____________.

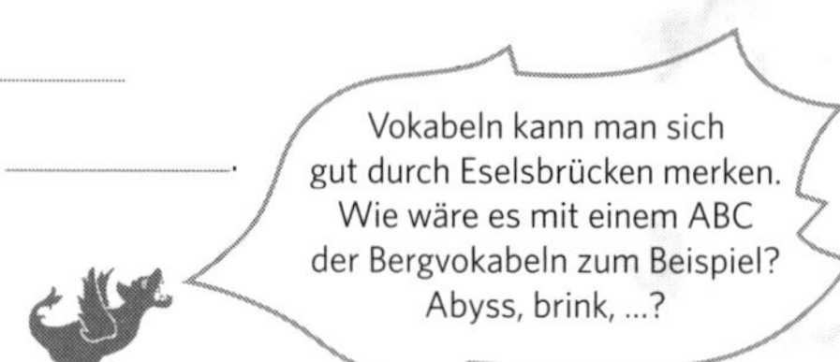

4 - Sarantuya appears

Meistens ist Sarantuya für Timucin nur zu hören, nur im Traum sieht er sie. Dennoch erscheint sie ihm nun auf dem Heiligen Berg. Prüfe folgende Aussagen zu ihrer Erscheinung auf ihre Richtigkeit.

		richtig	falsch
1.	This is the first time that Timucin really hears her voice.	☐	☐
2.	Sarantuya's scales are gold and she is gigantic.	☐	☐
3.	The dragon's face can show expressions like surprise.	☐	☐
4.	Timucin is not afraid of the dragon at all.	☐	☐
5.	The dragon disappears as he is looking at her.	☐	☐

The Lonely Warrior

5 - Mountain darkness

In diesem Textausschnitt über Timucins Rückweg bergab sind einige Wörter im Zwielicht des abendlichen Schneesturms nicht sofort erkennbar. Wähle die richtige Variante, um die Sätze zu vervollständigen.

Although his sense of direction is good, (1) shared/shaped/shaded by his life on the steppe, he has trouble finding his way in this empty (2) wasteland/watchman/wastespace.

The cold has followed him on his path from the top of the mountain, as well as the (3) darkness/dinginess/dimness which makes every step more dangerous than the last.

(4) Nightmare/Nightgown/Nightfall has brought thick, low cloud cover which obscures the moon and stars and fills the air with snow.

6 – Brother

Chuzir und Timucin sind Schwurbrüder und sind daher Verbündete bis zum Tod. Vervollständige diese Beschreibungen ihres besonderen Verhältnisses zueinander mit dem passenden Begriff. Übersetze dann diese Begriffe ins Deutsche!

1. Timucin and Chuzir swore one of these to each other.	a) treachery	
2. Chuzir carried this out when he broke his promise.	b) loyalty	
3. Chuzir asked Timucin for this after his betrayal.	c) oath	
4. Timucin now expects this from Chuzir.	d) forgiveness	

7 – Imperceptible

Im Dunkeln schleicht sich Üdschins Bande an Chuzir und Timucin heran. Dabei kommen Wörter vor, die mit Unsichtbarkeit und Unhörbarkeit zu tun haben. Findest du diese schleichenden Wörter hier in der Buchstabenmenge?

troyunheardgaffinvisiblemaclureunseenphoceainaudiblepirimperceptibleeaus

Was heißt das Wort im Aufgabentitel, *imperceptible*, auf Deutsch?

Im Englischen gibt es sowohl *un-* als auch *in-/im-* als Negativpräfixe. Z. B. *unseen*, aber *invisible*. Oft (aber nicht immer) wird *in-/im-* mit Wörtern verwendet, die aus dem Lateinischen stammen.

Help Arrives

8 - Ghosts from the past

In diesem Kapitel trifft Timucin zwei wichtige Menschen aus seiner Vergangenheit. Sind diese Aussagen dazu richtig oder falsch?

	richtig	falsch
1. Timucin thought that his mother was dead.	☐	☐
2. Chuzir attacks Üdschin with his sword and they fight.	☐	☐
3. Timucin is surprised to see Ilhan with his mother.	☐	☐
4. Ilhan is one of the tribe's most loyal warriors.	☐	☐

9 - Looking for someone

Durch die Steppe galoppieren Feinde, suchen sich Verwandte und verstecken sich Verfolgte. Fülle die Lücken in diesen Sätzen mit den Vokabeln rund ums Suchen, Finden und Fliehen.

hide · tracks · cover · looked · finds · flee · searching · chasing

Üdschin (1) ________ for her lost son for years, now she (2) ________ him.

The Tajin are (3) ________ Timucin and Chuzir, trying to follow their (4) ________ in the snow. Üdschin's men are outnumbered and must (5) ________ the Tajin instead of fighting. To (6) ________ from the Tajin, Üdschin's men must try to (7) ________ their tracks. Timucin and his mother are desperately (8) ________ for a safe place to stay.

Für die nächste Aufgabe:
Weißt du noch, wann *to* und wann *too* verwendet wird? *To* kommt mit Verben *(I want to go.)* oder als Präposition *(Come to my house.)* vor. *Too* heißt „zu viel" – *I'm too tired to come.* – oder „auch" – *I like that too.*

10 – Allegiance

For und *to* kommen im Englischen sehr häufig vor. Kannst du sie in diesem Text über Treue, Verrat und Verzeihung richtig einsetzen? An einigen Stellen kann es allerdings sein, das weder *for* noch *to* nötig ist – lass in dem Fall die Lücke leer.

"He has paid (1) ______ *this mistake. He knows he did wrong and has given me his word and begged* (2) ______ *forgiveness", grants Üdschin. "And that makes everything fine?" says Timucin bitterly. "No", replies his mother, "but being Khan means more than just having power, Timucin. It means that you must take responsibility* (3) ______ *all of those who swear allegiance* (4) ______ *you, for they are ready to give their lives* (5) ______ *you."*

The Smell of Blood

11 – Battle!

Es kommt zu einer erbitterten Schlacht zwischen Üdschins Männern und den Tajin. Wie viele englische Wörter zu diesem Thema lassen sich im Wirrwarr des Kampfes finden? Suche im Wortgitter und bedenke, dass die Wörter auch rückwärts oder diagonal laufen können.

W	O	R	R	A	A	T	B	O	W
E	I	C	B	D	E	J	O	K	O
A	G	S	C	V	N	E	X	A	U
P	D	C	D	S	C	E	E	R	N
O	O	O	J	W	T	I	F	T	D
N	O	F	B	O	I	H	E	E	E
O	L	F	R	R	E	G	G	A	D
M	B	L	A	D	E	W	F	I	F
T	N	N	A	U	T	Y	X	U	F
W	S	G	R	O	I	R	R	A	W

12 – Treacherous treachery

In dieser Erzählung kommen viele Wortstämme doppelt vor – einmal als Substantiv und einmal als Adjektiv (also wie *Wut* und *wütend* auf Deutsch). Bilde in dieser Übung entweder das Substantiv oder das Adjektiv zu dem jeweiligen Wort – die Wörter hast du im Kapitel gelesen.

Substantiv	Adjektiv
____________	wounded
____________	treacherous
ghost	____________
trap	____________

13 – Death

In diesem Kapitel sterben einige von Üdschins Männer sowie ein Tajin-Krieger. Welches Wort passt nicht in der Reihe zu diesem Thema – und warum?

to die | to perish | to kill | to take | dead | a life

____

The Secret Girlfriend

14 – Illness

Nach seiner Verletzung in der Schlacht leidet Chuzir unter einem furchtbaren Fieber. Kannst du die Begriffe, die sein Elend beschreiben, mit den deutschen Übersetzungen zusammenbringen?

1. fever	a) sich hin und her werfen
2. to hallucinate	b) Fieber
3. to toss and turn	c) brennen
4. pale	d) halluzinieren
5. to burn	e) blass

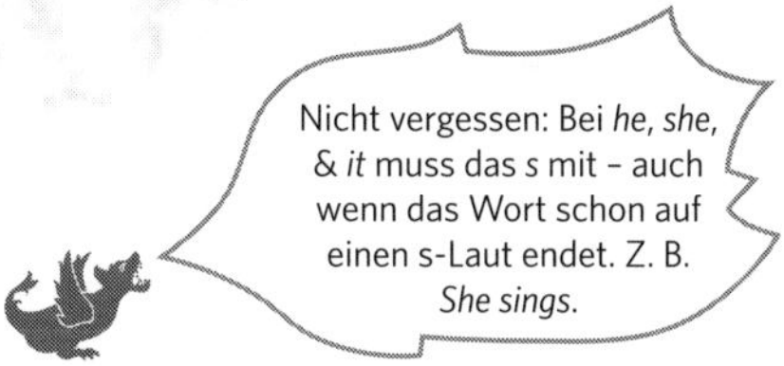

15 – Bruises and pains

Timucin schläft auf dem Berg und merkt erst, als er wieder wach wird, wie weh ihm sein Gesicht tut. Lies diesen Auszug zu dem Thema und entziffere die Anagramme an den Stellen, wo die Wörter fehlen.

He sshgi (1) ________ *as his head and shoulders fall forward, tsigr* (2) ________ *his teeth to stop himself sighing more and draws his cover closer around his shoulders. His face thurs* (3) ________ *so badly, so he carefully slefe* (4) ________ *it with the tips of his fingers; he is in pain, but everything essem* (5) ________ *to be where it should be, even if it doesn't feel like it used to.*

The Traitor

16 – Fire!

In Ilhan brennt ein feuriger Hass auf Timucin. Wörter, die mit Feuer zu tun haben, findest du hier in Anagramform. Entschlüssele die Anagramme und ordne dann das Ergebnis der passenden Übersetzung zu.

1. MOULDSER	S________	a) weißglühend
2. RUNB	B________	b) Brand
3. TOH HWIET	W________ H______	c) glimmen
4. EZBLA	B________	d) Glut
5. BRESEM	E ________	e) brennen

17 – Weaponry

Um eine Drohung zu verdeutlichen, lässt Ilhan gerne seine Hand auf seinen Schwertgriff fallen. Kannst du das Schwert mit den passenden Vokabeln genau beschriften?

1) Heft/Griff, 2) Schwert, 3) Klinge, 4) Spitze

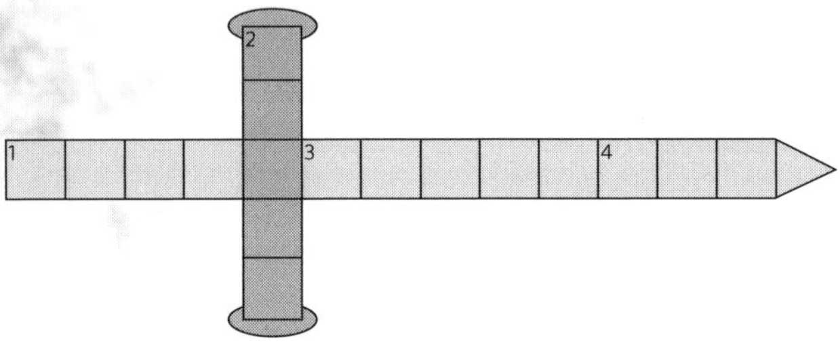

Kennst du auch einen anderen, moderneren Begriff für das Wort Nummer 1?

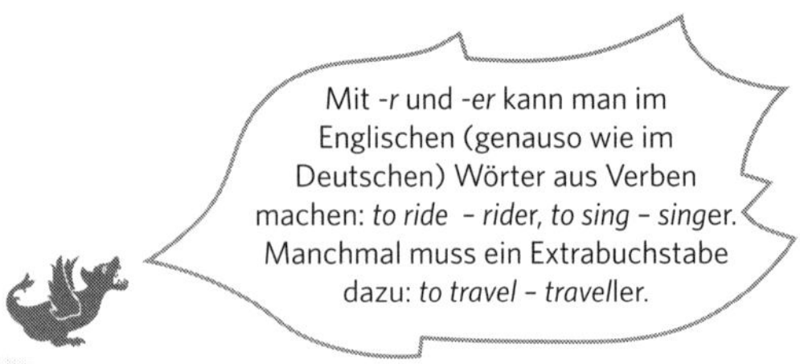

18 – Leadership

In diesem Kapitel verrät Üdschin ihrem Sohn Timucin einige Lebensweisheiten über Führung und Respekt. Kannst du die Vokabeln dazu in der Wortschlange auf der nächsten Seite finden?

The Shadow

19 – Trapped

Üdschin und ihre Männer sind auf dem Berg in einer Art sicheren Falle, in der sie unangreifbar sind, aus der sie aber auch nicht herauskommen. Prüfe diese Sätze zu ihrer schwierigen Lage und entscheide, ob sie richtig oder falsch sind.

	richtig	falsch
1. Üdschin and her warriors can defend the mountaintop easily.	☐	☐
2. The Tajin can fire arrows at them whilst they shelter on the peak.	☐	☐
3. The mountaintop is covered with trees for firewood.	☐	☐
4. Üdschin and her warriors are running out of food fast.	☐	☐
5. They discover a secret way down the mountain and avoid the Tajin.	☐	☐

20 – The Dragon's Rage

Timucin hat einen Alptraum, in dem ihm die Wut des Drachen vor Augen geführt wird. Zwischen der dunklen, mit Rauchschwaden durchzogenen Traumwelt und der Niederschrift sind einige Begriffe verschwommen: Bring die Buchstaben wieder in Ordnung!

The land starts to smoke, the slelm (1) ______________ of death is on the air. Where there were crystal-clear waters and summer loewrfs (2) ______________ of all colours, now armies march and make the earth shake. The black forces roll across the sapcaeldn (3) ______________ laying waste to whatever comes into their path. Fire and war harrow the country and yet the dragon is still in fury; wherever its adshow (4) ______________ touches the ground, all life is sedytroed (5) ______________ .

21 – Ransom

Hätte Üdschin für Timucin Lösegeld bezahlt? Das werden wir nie wissen. Füll dieses Wortgitter mit Buchstaben, um ein Lösegeld für Timucin aufzutreiben.

			R				
	W			L	T	H	
K	I				P		
P	R				N	E	R
		B			N	D	S
			M				

Im Englischen werden Titel wie **khan** oder **king** nur in der Anrede großgeschrieben. So heißt es zum Beispiel „What do you mean, my Khan?“, aber „He ist khan of the Voshon tribe.“

The Fight

22- Fight or flight?

Weil die Tajin geflüchtet sind, fallen in diesem Kapitel viele Wörter, die sich auf das Verlassen oder das Fliehen beziehen. Bring sie mit der richtigen deutschen Übersetzung zusammen.

1. to be gone	a) zurücklassen
2. to flee	b) weg sein
3. to leave	c) flüchten
4. to leave behind	d) verlassen

23 - Questions of authority

Timucin und Ilhan streiten sich. Dabei will jeder was von dem Vorhaben des anderen erfahren und stellt viele Fragen. Die Wörter, die sie brauchen, um Fragen zu stellen, befinden sich unten: Benutze sie, um die Lücken in den Fragesätzen zu füllen!

1. You think you should be Khan, ______________?
2. ______________ you rather wait here for them to come back?
3. You are afraid that my mother will make me Khan, ______________?
4. ______________ do you mean, 'like this'?
5. ______________ you dissatisfied with the order I gave?
6. ______________ should they trust you?

are | what | don't you | aren't you | why | would

The Way of the Warrior

24 - Crossword Puzzle

Löse dieses Kreuzworträtsel mit Vokabeln aus der ganzen Geschichte!

Across

1. Schwert
5. Festung
8. Krieger
10. Verführung

Down

2. Dolch
3. Heiliger Berg
4. Verräter
6. Barbaren
7. Stamm
9. Drache

The Decision

25 – Friendly unfriendliness

Die Welt des jungen Khans Timucin steckt voller Widersprüche. Dies führt unter anderem zu widersprüchlichen Formulierungen, Sachen, die nicht zueinander passen, wie „offenes Geheimnis" oder „dunkles Licht". Welche von den Wortpaarungen aus diesem Kapitel unten bildet ein solches Oxymoron?

friendly scorn

scornful answer

brave warrior

delicious vegetable

Lösungen

Brothers in Oath

1 - Tribe life

1-d, 2-e, 3-b, 4-a, 5-c

2 - The Holy Mountain

Sacred, ein Synonym ist übrigens holy.

3 - On the brink

1-edge *(Rand)*, 2-abyss *(Abgrund)*, 3-grip *(Halt)*, brink *(Rand)*

4 - Sarantuya appears

1-f, 2-r, 3-r, 4-f, 5-f

The Lonely Warrior

5 - Mountain darkness

1) shaped, 2) wasteland, 3) darkness, 4) nightfall

6 - Brothers

1-c, 2-a, 3-d, 4-b

treachery - Verrat, loyalty - Treue, oath - Eid, forgiveness - Verzeihung

7 - Imperceptible

unheard, invisible, unseen, inaudible; imperceptible - *unmerklich*

Help arrives

8 - Ghosts from the past

1-r, 2-f, 3-r, 4-f

9 - Looking for someone

1) looked, 2) finds, 3) chasing, 4) tracks, 5) flee, 6) hide, 7) cover , 8) searching

10 - Allegiance

1) for, 2) - , 3) for, 4) to, 5) for

The Smell of Blood

11 - Battle!

Arrow, bow, wounded, weapon, dagger, sword, fight, blade, blood, defend, warrior.

W	O	R	R	A	A	T	B	O	W
E	I	C	B	D	E	J	O	K	O
A	G	S	C	V	N	E	X	A	U
P	D	C	D	S	C	E	E	R	N
O	O	O	J	W	T	I	F	T	D
N	O	F	B	O	I	H	E	E	E
O	L	F	R	R	E	G	G	A	D
M	B	L	A	D	E	W	F	I	F
T	N	N	A	U	T	Y	X	U	F
W	S	G	R	O	I	R	R	A	W

12 - Treacherous treachery

Wound - wounded; traitor - treacherous; ghost - ghostly; trap - trapped

13 - Death

dead - alle andere Wörter sind Verben

The Secret Girlfriend

14 - Ilness

1-b, 2-d, 3-a, 4-e, 5-c

15 - Bruises and pains

1) sighs, 2) grits, 3) hurts, 4) feels, 5) seems

The Traitor

16 – Fire!

1) smoulder - c, 2) burn - e,
3) white hot - a, 4) blaze - Brand,
5) embers - Glut

17 – Weaponry

1. hilt, 2. sword, 3. blade, 4. Tipp

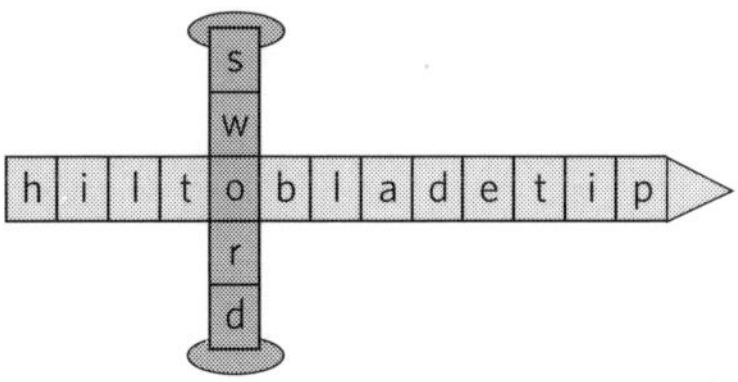

Ein anderes Wort für *hilt* ist *handle.*

18 – Leadership

Respect *(Respekt, Achtung)*, followers *(Gefolgsmänner/-leute)*, trust *(Vertrauen)*, generous *(großzügig)*, leader *(Anführer)*

The Shadow

19 – Trapped

1-r, 2-f, 3-f, 4-r, 5-f

20 – The Dragon's Rage

1) smell, 2) flowers, 3) landscape,
4) shadow, 5) destroyed

21 – Ransom

Wealth *(Reichtum)*, kidnap *(entführen)*, prisoner *(Gefangener)*, bounds *(Grenzen)*, ransom *(Lösegeld)*

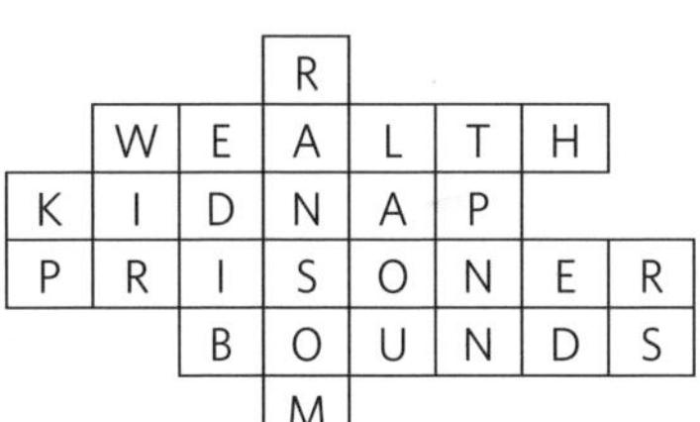

The Fight

22 – Fight or flight?

1-b, 2-c, 3-d, 4-a

23 – Questions of authority

1-don't you, 2-would, 3-aren't you,
4-what, 5-are, 6-why

The Way of the Warrior

24 – Crossword Puzzle

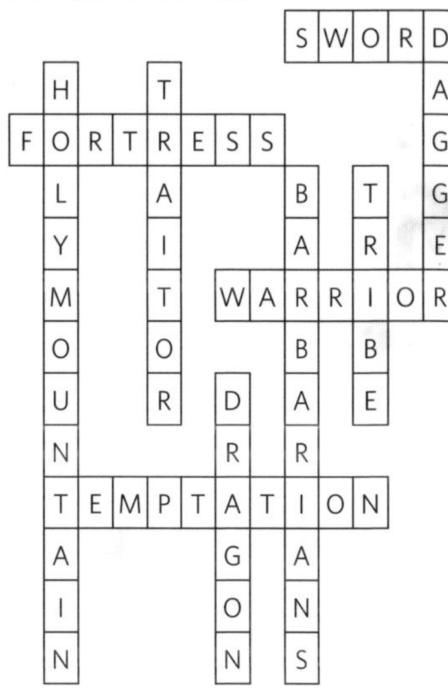

Across

1. Schwert - sword
5. Festung - fortress
8. Krieger - warrior
10. Verführung - temptation

Down

2. Dolch - dagger
3. Heiliger Berg - Holy Mountain
4. Verräter - traitor
6. Barbaren - barbarians
7. Stamm - tribe
9. Drache - dragon

The Decision

25 - Friendly unfriendlyness

Friendly scorn; das bedeutet *freundliche Verachtung*.

Drachenfragen und -antworten

The Prophecy
Which face from his past does Timucin see in a vision?
Welches Gesicht aus seiner Vergangenheit sieht Timucin in einer Vision?
Timucin sieht Arbesa, das Mädchen, das ihm als Braut versprochen wurde und in das er sich verliebt hat. Sie wurde allerdings von Feinden ihrer beider Klans gefangengenommen.

The Lonely Warrior
What is the special connection between Chuzir and Timucin?
Welche besondere Verbindung besteht zwischen Chuzir und Timucin?
Chuzir und Timucin sind Schwurbrüder: Sie haben einen Eid abgelegt, dass sie füreinander einstehen. Sie stehen sich damit näher als Brüder.

Help Arrives
According to Üdschin, what is the most important thing a Khan has to do?
Was ist laut Timucins Mutter Üdschin das Wichtigste, das ein Khan tun muss?
Üdschin sieht es höchste Pflicht eines Khans an, seinen Gefolgsmänner zu verzeihen.

The Smell of Blood
Whose idea is it to retreat to the peak of the Holy Mountain – and why?
Wessen Idee ist es, dass die Krieger sich auf den Gipfel des Heiligen Bergs zurückziehen, und warum?
Timucin schlägt vor, dass sie sich auf den Berg zurückziehen, weil man ihn mit wenigen Kriegern gegen viele verteidigen kann.

The Secret Girlfriend
Why is Timucin so embarrassed about having mentioned Sarantuya?
Warum ist es Timucin so peinlich, dass er Sarantuya erwähnt hat?
Timucin will nicht erklären müssen, dass er sich in Gedanken oft mit einem Drachen unterhält, der ihm in seiner Gedankenwelt erscheint. Er denkt, dass die anderen ihn dann nicht mehr ernst nehmen. Zudem interessiert sich seine Mutter naturgemäß für alle weibliche Namen, die er fallen lässt, und stellt peinliche Fragen.

The Traitor

Where do Üdschin's fighting men come from and why do they follow her?

Woher kommen Üdschins Krieger und weshalb folgen sie ihr?

Üdschins Gefolgschaft besteht aus Merkiten. Sie selbst ist von diesem Stamm. Die Männer wurden ihr vom Stammesführer zur Verfügung gestellt, damit sie ihr helfen, ihren Sohn zu befreien. Da die Männer ihrem Khan treu dienen, folgen sie auf seinen Befehl hin Üdschin.

The Shadow

What is Sarantuya trying to show Timucin in the nightmare he has?

Was versucht Sarantuya Timucin durch seinen Albtraum zu zeigen?

Sarantuya zeigt Timucin die Zerstörung und das Leiden, die der Krieg mit sich bringen. Sollte er den Weg des Drachen wählen, so wird er für die Verheerung des grünen Landes jenseits des Berges verantwortlich sein.

The Fight

Why do the Tajin not attack them as they leave the mountain?

Warum greifen die Tajin Timucin und die anderen Krieger nicht an, als sie den Berg verlassen?

Die Tajin sind aus unbekannten Gründen geflüchtet, wie Timucin und Ihan merken, als sie den Lagerplatz untersuchen. Deswegen können sie unbehelligt vom Berg herunterkommen.

The Way of the Warrior

Who does Timucin think the horsemen are as he lays down his weapons?

Was glaubt Timucin, wer die Reiter sind, als er seine Waffen niederlegt?

Timucin hält die Merkiten für Tajin und will sich diesen ergeben, damit Üdschin und ihren Kriegern den Tod erspart bleibt.

The Decision

What does everyone expect Timucin to do with the baby and why?

Was erwarten alle: was soll Timucin mit Arbesas Kind tun und warum?

Es wird von Timucin erwartet, dass er Arbesas Kind tötet, wenn er sie heiraten will. Da das Kind von einem Tajin oder einem der Barbaren aus dem Norden stammt, gilt es als Sache der Ehre für Timucin, das Kind aus dem Weg zu räumen.

Weitere Drachenabenteuer von Wolfgang Hohlbein

**PONS Wolfgang Hohlbein -
Age of Dragons + MP3-CD**

Timucin hat keinen leichten Stand im Klan. Die anderen Jungkrieger machen ihm das Leben schwer, denn im Bogenschießen und im Schwertkampf ist er nur Mittelmaß. Zudem hat er panische Angst vor Hunden, obwohl der Hund doch der engste Freund eines jeden Kriegers ist! Sogar Timucins Schwurbruder Chuzir fällt ihm in den Rücken und verbündet sich mit seinen Gegnern. Doch Timucin hat ein besonderes Geheimnis: Nachts bekommt er Besuch von einem rätselhaften Drachen. Dann lernt er die stolze Arbesa kennen – und muss sich schließlich der schwersten aller Prüfungen stellen.

Format: 13,5 x 19,5 cm

Ca. 128 Seiten, Broschur

ISBN: 978-3-12-010070-6

**PONS Wolfgang Hohlbein -
Dream of Dragons + MP3-CD**

Timucin erlebt neue Abenteuer! Auf der halsbrecherischen Flucht vor seinen erbarmungslosen Feinden muss Timucin sich beweisen, ohne Freunde und Kampfgefährten. Nur begleitet von seiner Verlobten Arbesa und seiner Mutter schlägt er sich durch den eisigen Winter der Steppe. Und ihre Feinde rücken immer näher. Timucin hat nur ein Ziel vor Augen: er muss den Heiligen Berg erreichen und dort die rettende Hilfe finden, ohne die sie verloren sind.

Doch dann gerät er plötzlich in Gefangenschaft! Kann er seinen grausamen Wärtern entkommen?

Format: 13,5 x 19,5 cm

Ca. 128 Seiten, Broschur

ISBN: 978-3-12-010071-3

PONS

www.pons.de